# Advance Praise for
# Victim Is Not Your Name

"Coming from over thirty years in the personal development field, I know that stepping out of a victim role is critical to creating a life of joy and possibility. In Victim Is Not Your Name, Kelly Bennett makes an amazing case for the need to make that transition, the certainty it can be done, along with practical advice on how to accomplish it...all powerful messages. Kelly knows what she is talking about, pure and simple. Her years of working with people who have dealt with pain, abuse, trauma and more makes her uniquely qualified to help anyone see the path out of pain by doing the inner work of taking back their power. Through her 'tell it like it is' and yet deeply caring approach to this sensitive subject, Kelly offers sage advice that is clear and effective.

Every aspect of Victim Is Not Your Name is engaging—from the introduction of the power a name can have, through how Victim Habits can take over and even take you down, to step-by-step, practical advice on how to take back your life. Read this book if you feel stuck, if you feel someone or something has harmed you and you don't know how to get past it in order live the life and feel the happiness and joy you deserve. Read this book if regardless of what has happened in your life, you are ready to live fully, live powerfully. Read this book if you are ready to create a compelling future for yourself and the people you love."

~ DEBRA RUSSELL,
Strengths-Based Performance Coach – Debra Russell Coaching and author, *I Almost Missed My Life...Don't Miss Yours,*
Master/Platinum Coach for the Tony Robbins Companies, former Head Trainer and General Manager for Robbins Research International

"Kelly Bennett's Victim is Not Your Name is a very helpful resource to people who have been unjustly injured. Her practical suggestions mixed with anecdotes from personal experience create a book that is easy to read and very useful to anyone who is stuck after a serious setback. I gladly recommend it."

~ PROFESSOR PETER ROBINSON
Pepperdine University Caruso School of Law and author of *Apology, Forgiveness, and Reconciliation for Good Lawyers and Other Peacemakers*

"Victim Is Not Your Name is a straightforward, practical approach to taking your life back when in crisis. Kelly Bennett provides nonjudgmental, empathetic tools to guide others through their challenging journey in a way that is not only hopeful, but necessary, in a world wrought with turmoil, fear, and victim-inducing circumstances. Kelly's credentials as a crisis manager for decades gives her a wealth of valid experiences to draw from. Anyone who is currently facing a challenge or has a loved one that is, as well as church leaders, school teachers, community leaders, youth advisors, law enforcement, crisis managers—just about anyone can benefit by learning to recognize and move through or help someone else move through victimization."

~ HON. SHERRILL A. ELLSWORTH (RET.),
Past Presiding Judge of Riverside County
Superior Court, CA and co-founder of coParenter.com

"Self-help books often lack the ability to communicate effectively due to social or psychological jargon. Kelly Bennett's down to earth stories about real people, in a straightforward conversational way, give you the feeling that you are sitting across the table talking to her. Ms. Bennett is an intelligent, articulate, experienced attorney and mediator, whose life of service to clients enables her to see how best to resolve the problems that the label 'victim' carries. The incredible insights in this book are applicable to just about anybody—it's about the ability to see beyond the immediate circumstances and to grow your inner strengths."

~ COLONEL RICK GIBBS (Ret.), United States Air Force,
Mayor Emeritus City of Murrieta, CA, Businessman

"Victim Is Not Your Name is highly engaging and an easy read, but don't misunderstand; it is full of life changing golden nuggets for all of us. The applications target living life to the fullest, as well as overcoming the adversities of victimhood—something many of us have experienced and I dare say, all of us have dealt with. Kelly Bennett's work has inspired me to, among other things, throw some stuff away, breathe, and yes, I've got a gratitude stone I'm going to start carrying with me. This book also reinforced my commitment to, first thing in morning, read the Word, pray, and think great thoughts!"

~ DENNIS G. BREWER, JR., ESQ.,
General Counsel and CFO, Fellowship Church
and C3Global, Grapevine, TX;
Founding Partner, Brewer, Lang, Veach, Irving, TX

"Victim Is Not Your Name should be required reading for all of us. Don't we all, at times, find ourselves slipping into feeling sorry for ourselves? Wallowing in self-pity? Kelly Bennett reminds us that we have a choice in whether we are to remain victims. Over the past thirty-five years in the legal profession, I have worked with countless victims. Many have been female sexual assault victims. Others are male combat veterans suffering from severe PTSD and depression. I can tell you, Kelly's advice is spot on. People get trapped in a perception of themselves as a victim. They never move on. Kelly gives them the tools to do that. I know Kelly personally and have sought her for advice at trying times in my life. She is one of the best lawyers in California and a first class mediator. Few could deliver this message with the humility and authority she does. I particularly loved the chapter on forgiveness, and Kelly's words: 'Forgiveness is an amazing gift you give to yourself--a freeing of the soul.' Lovely."

~ JUDGE OF THE SUPERIOR COURT, CALIFORNIA

"Victim Is Not Your Name provides a roadmap to regain your confidence, identity and productivity. Particularly impactful is Kelly Bennett's discussion about how in some cases, the victim identity can be a comfortable one—an insight that is uncomfortably accurate. Kelly allows the reader to acknowledge where they are in life, and if they are true to themselves, she provides the steps to follow for freedom. Victim Is Not Your Name is a must read—it provides a meaningful path forward. This book should be read by anyone who is interested in helping themselves or others move forward, regain their identity and confidence, and begin—again—to find their purpose and seek their potential."

~ RICK BISHOP, Executive Director
Western Riverside Council of Governments,
Riverside County Habitat Conservation Agency,
Western Community Energy, CA

"Victim Is Not Your Name is a breath of fresh air. This message for victims and those who counsel them is nothing short of inspiring. Kelly Bennett is relentless in her pursuit of truth, answering the hard questions, not in a judgmental or presumptuous tone but in a manner that fully understands the breadth and complexities of suffering. Victim Is Not Your Name inspires us to realize that we are much more than what happens to us.  We are not simply byproducts of our circumstances.  We can and will overcome by having the right focus and right attitude. Anyone who identifies with being a true friend, loved one, mother, father, husband, wife, son, daughter, teacher, or counselor should read this book."

~ COURTNEY COATES, Attorney and Pastor,
Principal and Founder of the Law Office of
Courtney M. Coates, Temecula, CA

# Victim Is Not Your Name

### Remembering Your True Identity
### In the Midst of Life Challenges

## Kelly A. Bennett, Esq.

Law Love Life Books®

You were remarkably and  wonderfully made.

You were made with an indelible,

unchangeable identity.

An identity inspired by, and based upon,

the image of your Creator.

An identity designed for fulfillment,

greatness, and purpose.


There's only one True You.

Let not the world, nor its circumstances,

tell you otherwise.


Kelly A. Bennett, Esq.

Copyright © 2019 by Kelly A. Bennett.

All rights reserved. Published in the United States by Law Love Life Books®, a division of Law Love Life International, Inc., California. lawlovelifebooks.com

Law Love Life Books® is a trademark, and the Law Love Life Books® logo is a trademark of Law Love Life International, Inc.

Library of Congress Cataloging-in-Publication data is available upon request.

ISBN: 9781671294462

Cover design and inside art by Jose Bono
Cover image by Taylor Brooks

**vic·tim** _____

ˈviktəm

> a person harmed, injured, or killed as a result of a crime, accident, or other event or action.*

**vic·tor** _____

ˈviktər

> a person who defeats an enemy or opponent in a battle, game or other competition.*

**name** _____

nām

1. a word or set of words by which a person, animal, place, or thing is known, addressed, or referred to.*

2. a famous person.*

**i·den·ti·ty** _____

īden(t)ədē

1. the fact of being who or what a person or this is.*

2. a close similarity or affinity.*

3. a transformation that leaves an object unchanged.*

4. the equality of two expressions for all values of the quantities expressed by letters, or an equation expressing this, e.g. $(x + 1)2 = x2 + 2x +1$.*

_____

* Lexico.com, powered by Oxford University Press (2019)

# Dedication

*To the brokenhearted and downtrodden.*
*You are the victors of the future.*

# Contents

# An Introduction Worth Reading
## (Don't Skip This)

L ife's thrown challenges your way, leaving you feeling used up, exhausted. Maybe angry, maybe depressed. In short, you feel like a victim...of a wrongdoer, of circumstance or both. You know intuitively that you cannot survive and thrive in your current condition. Life just isn't meant to be this way.

You're tired of the grind—slogging forward, day by day, living with losses and pain that seem too high to ever overcome. But here's the good news: You don't have to keep living this way. There is a way out, and your life *can* get better—*much better.*

The villain in your story is called the Victim Habit. The villain is neither the person nor the circumstance that harmed you. The Victim Habit is how you define yourself. It is a way of being, a pattern of behaviors you developed *in response* to the harms you've suffered. The Victim Habit creates roadblocks in your relationships with the people you need most. It sells you a bill of goods, convincing you that you're someone you're not. The Victim Habit leaves you feeling hopeless and helpless, questioning your values and everything that you previously believed to be good and true.

My life's work thus far has been an enormous privilege, one where I've stood shoulder-to-shoulder with beautiful souls who've endured pain at the hands of others and unexpected circumstances. I've watched the Victim Habit in action, and my heart hurts at the suffering going on. I want you to know that your suffering *doesn't have to be a life sentence*.

Over the last 30 years, I've worked as a trial lawyer. I've worked as a business lawyer counseling entrepreneurs starting and growing their companies. I've represented business owners and organizational leaders in the midst of serious and complicated problems (sometimes quite personal) where the viability of their life's work was at risk. I've worked heavily in family law, negotiating, mediating and litigating for people who've had some really horrible (sometimes unthinkable) things happen; betrayals by those they trusted most. Many found themselves starting all over again. And I've served as an elected official, a mayor and a regional government leader, creating systems and processes for productivity, attaining lofty goals and solving large-scale problems.

Working so heavily in the people and problems business, I've learned a lot about the human ability to survive and thrive *as a result of* adversity. Feeling safe, living with certainty that you are not only going to be OK but *well*, is within your reach. Becoming free of the burdensome thoughts that preoccupy your mind is possible. Discovering your worth, your purpose and your future is possible. You are not alone in your pain. Deep, healthy connections with others and restoring love into your daily life are available to you—and they will come.

This book presents a plan for eradicating the Victim Habit. It is a process to move you out of discontentedness and into a place of peace. It provides tools to up-level you into a life of significance, joy-filled experiences and hopefulness. These tools come from those many years of experience and service to others that I've been so privileged to have. The plan also leverages the knowledge of many other experts who have also helped people move through crises.

Now for the ask: I invite you to agree, in advance, that you'll take in the information and the plan presented here with an open mind. Look for yourself within these pages. I will challenge you and call you to move forward. With courage and action, you'll begin to transform your life from stalled-out to fired-up. Do nothing and you'll stay "stuck." Do nothing and you'll miss out on key opportunities that are waiting for you. But you're not a do-nothing kind of person... you're already moving forward by reading this book. Transformation is yours for the taking, and you're on your way.

The support and enthusiasm around this book has been incredible. I am thrilled and simultaneously humbled by the outpouring of love and encouragement from my trusted inner circle and my friends in the community.

For you dear reader, my prayer is that the ideas presented here will *inspire* you, *encourage* you and *ignite* in you the radical courage to reach for the stars, no matter what life has lobbed your way. And as you reach for those stars, the watching world will benefit from all you were made to be.

~ KB

# PART ONE

## WHY NAMES MATTER

-----------------------------------------

# 1

# "Victim" Is An Adjective—Not A Name

**To know who you are is the greatest power of all.**

*Sherrilyn Kenyon and Dianna Love, Blood Trinity*

On a balmy August evening in 1989, a most unlikely scene unfolded in Beverly Hills, a tony suburb of Los Angeles, California. Two brothers ages 18 and 21, armed with 12 gauge shotguns burst into the den of their family home (a 9,000 square foot mansion), murdering their parents at point-blank range. Over the next six months, the brothers lived the high life, spending approximately $1 million on clothes, vacations, penthouses and tennis coaches.

The privileged, well-educated Menendez brothers tried to excuse their crimes, entering not-guilty pleas. The brothers said they acted in self-defense (even though their parents were watching television at the time of the murders), and that they were victims of years of sexual and physical abuse by both of their parents. A jury eventually convicted the brothers of two counts each of first degree murder with special circumstances, and conspiracy to commit murder. They were sentenced to life in prison, without the possibility of parole.

There is no freedom without responsibility. To this day, Lyle and Erik Menendez refuse to take responsibility for killing their parents. They've adopted a seemingly permanent victim identity, which has them stuck in an unending loop of blaming. As a result of their refusal to accept responsibility for their heinous crimes, the brothers will never experience freedom outside of prison walls.

Were the boys severely abused as they claimed? Who knows, perhaps. But one thing's for sure—they adopted a victim identity and it failed them, miserably.

The story of the Menendez brothers is extreme. But it makes the point that while circumstances may cause you to fit the adjective "victim," neither you nor the Menendez brothers were ever meant to *become* victims. The role of victim does not serve you long-term; instead, taking on victim as your name, your *persona,* is confining, sometimes for life.

When bad things happen, the world (the good and well-intentioned parts of the world) wants to label you, "victim." That label quietly shifts from an *adjective* to an *identity.* Well-meaning responses come from neighbors, churches, family and friends when bad things happen to us. Springing from a desire to help—as they imagine your pain—they give you the label of "victim." Our criminal courts call you the "victim." There are "victim impact statements" read during sentencing hearings for criminals. Most county prosecutors' offices have a "victim services" department. There are "victim advocates" that will go to court with "the victim," and many states have "victim compensation" programs.

The goal of programs and services designed for victims is laudable, and very much needed in most instances. However, despite the good intentions, these programs can unwittingly encourage the adoption of a new identity that in the long run doesn't really serve us. Not surprisingly, the adjective "victim" becomes an identity thief the moment our cognitive backs are turned.

A surprising number of people drift through life unconsciously, failing to challenge the adjectives...the labels others place on them. We easily accept external labels without much thought. As I looked at this common practice, I couldn't help but think, "Well why *wouldn't* we accept outside labels so easily? It's a *habit* started shortly after birth. How could this *not* be our default setting?"

Think about how impressionable you were as a young child, a time in your life when you most easily accepted the labels given to you by others. You didn't know any better. Your critical thinking skills had not fully developed. Without intervention, over time we go into "autopilot" and routinely accept external labels. Consider these common phrases heard during childhood:

"No, no, no! You're such a *bad girl*!"
"What's *wrong* with you!?"
"You're fat."
"You're so lazy!"
"You're ridiculous."
"OK, stupid!"
"You should be ashamed of yourself."
"You'll never amount to anything."

As children, most of us didn't know how to separate fact from fiction when an adult or popular kids labeled us. As adults, the habit continues until we know better, and learn a new pattern of listening, analyzing and responding. The great news is, the habit of blind label-acceptance isn't a life sentence. Cultivating a new habit is totally doable.

**The Power of the Name.** What *you* call yourself is a big deal. How *you* view yourself, and what you then *expect for yourself* is heavily influenced by the titles you allow to be placed on you. This is not a new idea, really. The names you adopt for yourself have powerful impacts on you. This is not just an idea. No, the truth of the matter is steeped in fact and proven in a myriad of social and psychological studies. The wise and the sage people in our culture understand the power of the name, and pass that understanding on to those who will slow down long enough to listen.

It was 2009, and I was in a courtroom on a hot August evening. Judge Carol Codrington was on the bench that night, volunteering during her "off duty" time for the local Youth Court here in Southern California. Youth Court is a diversion program where low-level teenage offenders get a chance to have their records wiped clean if they complete the program. The first step is for the teen to appear in open court, before a "jury" of her peers—other teens in the community—and admit to the crime. Next, the teen stands before the court and answers pointed questions from the teen-jury and the judge.

Judge Codrington is an extraordinarily intelligent jurist, known for her regal command of the courtroom. That night, an "offender" was standing before the judge, having committed a crime of deception. The teen attempted to lie to Judge Codrington, and got called out for it. Judge Codrington looked deep into the eyes of the young man and said (paraphrased from my keen recollection):

*You know, your **name**, and the **reputation** behind that name, is all you really have in this life. The good news is, **you get to decide** what that name is...**you decide** what that reputation is going to be.*

*Your reputation is defined by your actions. No one can take your name or your reputation away from you. But **you** can take away all that is good about it, by the way you decide to live. Value it. Treasure it. Because it's the most important thing.*

Judge Codrington was right. The core lesson was, you and I **get to decide** what our names *mean*. Oh, but please...be careful of the meaning you give it.

If I allow "Kelly Bennett" to *mean* "victim" or "disabled," my mind and my behavior will easily adopt that role. When you live with a limiting label, before you know it life is small, shallow, and short on hope. As Judge Codrington pointed out, reputation is built on how we behave. We'll always live up to (or tolerate) the reputation we create.

**Name Signaling.** A phenomenon called "name signaling" has been studied as far back as 1948. Name signaling is all about the societal signals a person's name communicates. Studies consistently reveal that names communicate messages about a person's ethnicity, socio-economic background, social status and spiritual beliefs. Traditionally, name signaling has been studied in the context of the *external*—what our names communicate *to others* in the society in which we live.

Years ago my husband and I relocated our home and our law practice from Orange County to Riverside County, California—just one county away. As we got to know the local legal community, the name "Melissa Sue Johnson" came up somewhat frequently. Although I had not yet met Melissa Sue, I heard other family law attorneys casually mention her in conversation. They spoke well of Melissa Sue, as a good family law attorney with whom they'd had cases. A few years later, I finally ran into Melissa Sue Johnson in person. It was an encounter I'll never forget.

I was at court one morning in the private attorney room when several lawyers walked in—one I did not recognize. I introduced myself, and to my surprise the friendly African American attorney held out her hand, and with a warm smile introduced herself as Melissa Sue

Johnson. She couldn't help but notice the shocked expression on my face. As we began to chat, Melissa Sue told me that she had been an attorney in Riverside County for many years, and decided to go by the name "Melissa Sue Johnson" for business purposes. You see, Riverside County has historically been an overtly conservative county, with a primarily Caucasian demographic.

Melissa Sue said that when she first hung out her shingle, she received very few calls in response to her local advertising where she'd used her real name. It was "too ethnic," she explained. So Melissa Sue decided to "skin that cat" by changing her name to a "Caucasian sounding" name. Regardless of what we think of this story, it worked. Melissa Sue started booking initial consultations and business began to boom. What happened to Melissa Sue was a classic instance of *name signaling* (not to mention absurd discrimination).

While name signaling has been studied in the context of how society views us *in response to* our names, what about the affect our own names have on how we view ourselves? If we associate meanings to names on an *external* basis, why wouldn't we also do this on an *internal* basis? In fact, we do.

*The New Yorker* columnist Maria Konnikova wrote about name signaling, citing a seven year study in a Florida school district. The Florida study revealed that a child's name had a direct affect on the teacher's expectations of the student, which in turn affected the student's expectations for themselves. This was proven by student performance and test scores. For example, the children whose names were associated with lower socio-economic status, and/or whose names were linked to "being black," were met with lower teacher expectations. Inherent biases arising out of name signaling were revealed, and the students with the "black" names and "poor" name signals performed at much lower levels than their counter-parts with non-black, non-poor status signals.[1]

We should not overlook the significance of name signaling—especially if you've experienced life traumas. If you allow yourself to be labeled a "victim," what do you think the long-term outcome will be on your life outlook, your performance levels and your expectations of yourself? It all depends, I suppose, on the *meaning* you assign to the name "victim." When you give yourself permission to identify as a victim, to the extent it becomes a *name* rather than an adjective, you run a great risk of limiting yourself. Like the Florida teachers who unconsciously had lower expectations of the "black-named students" and the "poor-culture students," adopting "victim" as your name may be the free pass you give yourself to tolerate mediocrity and shallow living.

**The Belief-Stress Connection.** In 2014, a group of researchers studied the correlation between beliefs and stress.[2] They examined a group of high school students' beliefs about whether a person's personality can change or not. Interestingly, the students who believed that personality characteristics *can* change experienced much lower stress levels, better health and higher grades. Those students who used terms to describe people (including themselves—such as *bully, nerd, athlete, victim*) and who believed that those people *cannot change*, experienced increased stress and much lower performance.

The belief-stress study revealed that we tend to label others and ourselves by the characteristics they/we routinely display. More importantly, the label we attach carries with it a *belief* that the behavior reflects a person's *intrinsic nature*. Why is this? Because each time someone mistreats us, we tend to conclude that their mistreatment is evidence that they're a bad person. Our internal dialogue doesn't say, "that's probably a good person who just happened to do a bad thing to me..." Instead most of us conclude, "That person tends to mistreat people, because they are *the kind of person* who mistreats people." This thinking applies to the labels we give ourselves. When we do this, our self-applied label not only reflects who we are in the moment, but also our *belief* about who we are *at our core*.[3] This default is called Labeling Theory.

**Bucking the Default for External Labels.** It's dangerous to accept the label "victim" from others, because once accepted, that external label is hard to shake. American social scientists have long studied the impacts societal labels have on people. This is where "Labeling Theory" emerged. Labeling Theory simply means that we begin to identify and behave in ways that reflect the labels society places upon us. Labeling Theory is most commonly debated in criminology and the study of deviant behavior (really, it's a fancy explanation for "self-fulfilling prophecies" and stereotyping).

Stick with me here. I'm not suggesting that the victim label will make you a deviant. What I am suggesting is that the sociology of deviancy has an important correlation to the victim label and our own internal self-talk around the "victim" reference. Sociological studies of crime and deviance established that labeling and treating a person as a "criminal" or a criminal "deviant" actually fosters negative, deviant behavior. When someone is labeled as a "criminal," that label causes others to treat that person more negatively. In response to that negative treatment, the "criminal" responds in negative, deviant ways.[4] It's a response to the stereotype.

Consider the military veteran who served in outrageously frightening combat zones, was raped by her fellow comrades, and returned home with extreme PTSD. It's no surprise when she turns to drinking and smoking weed to cope. After a while, she seeks a stronger drug to alleviate the chronic mental and physical pain inflicted by the PTSD and her experiences. Before she knows it, our veteran's got a heroin addiction and has lost her job. Of course, the addiction runs the typical cycle and our veteran resorts to breaking into cars to steal money and credit cards to fund her addiction and keep the pain at bay. You know the end of the story—she ultimately gets arrested, charged and convicted of the crimes associated with the behavior. If she's lucky, our veteran goes into drug programs through the VA and gets clean.

But now she's been labeled a criminal by the court and society. What happens when our clean, rehabilitated veteran now tries to get a job? With the criminal label, her veteran status holds less weight and she's treated negatively. In response to rejection after rejection (and the dire financial straits our drug-free veteran finds herself in, with no drug to help her "cope"), she goes back to the drugs and the stealing. She begins to believe the label "criminal" and adopts it as her identity. Think about how easily that label "criminal" makes it for our veteran to justify her behavior.

Just like our PTSD plagued veteran, Labeling Theory applies to us regardless of the label. How we respond to the labels has an enormous impact on our lives. When we adopt the descriptor "victim" as our name, as who we are, we set ourselves up to linger in a space of continual suffering.

**Self-Talk and Inconsistent Identities.** After years of working with people who indeed have been harmed by others, I've learned that we truly get what we set our focus on. Often, we unwittingly give ourselves mixed signals—aligning ourselves with multiple, incongruent identities; identities that we simply can't hold at the same time. The negative label immobilizes the positive label. I've watched, through hundreds of my law clients' experiences, the sad effects of people staying in that limiting space called "victim." It all goes back to that popular concept we've heard about for years called "negative self-talk." Is it real? You bet it is.

To understand the impact of the labels we self-talk ourselves into, it helps to think about the *meaning* we associate with the label. I'm very pragmatic, and not a super touchy-feely kind of gal (chalk it up to the lawyer in me), but there's truth to the idea that the *meanings* we give to words and labels strongly influence our state of mind...how we *feel*. When you put a label on yourself, you influence how you feel about yourself through the meaning you attach to the label. After several years of consciously paying attention to the words and labels I use, and how it *feels* when I use them, I've become a true believer in the power of the prose.

A number of years ago, I decided to hire a high-performance business coach. This was one of the smartest moves I've ever made (yes, if you're in business I recommend getting a coach—it's made a remarkable difference in my personal and career lives). In one of the very first sessions, I began expressing frustration to my coach, Debra. I was complaining about constantly feeling behind in my work and not achieving the goals that were truly important to me. I'll never forget this exchange:

| | |
|---|---|
| Me: | I'm so overwhelmed! I just can't get it all done! |
| Coach Debra: | Whoa, whoa, whoa. I'm going to stop you right there. I want you to really pay attention to the words you're using, because they are powerful. When you say you're 'so overwhelmed,' how does that make you feel? |
| Me: | [Internal thought bubble: 'Seriously Debra? How do I feel? I thought this was business coaching, not a shrink session...'] |
| | [Polite response...] Hmm, I'm not sure what you mean. |

Coach Debra: Sure you do. When you say you're 'so over-whelmed,' how do you feel inside? Energized? Encouraged? Light? Heavy? What?

Me: Well, I guess I feel...uggh. Heavy. Oppressed. Chaotic. Well, yeah...overall, stressed.

Coach Debra: Our words matter, because we attach *meanings* to them. So if you want to change your state to something that supports your success, you either don't use certain words or you change the meaning those words have.

Instead of telling yourself you're overwhelmed, let's look at the facts. The reality is, there are a lot of tasks you believe need to be completed. Let's break it down. List the tasks and ask, 'Are all these really important or necessary? What am I *not* going to do? What do I *want* to do or have done? Who else can do the tasks I want to have done?'

Instead of labeling yourself as 'overwhelmed' I encourage you to not label yourself with this at all.

Drop the mic. Cue the music. See the clouds part. It dawned on me right then and there...*I have a choice* about how I feel about myself. *I* choose my state of mind, and my identity. My self-talk really does make a difference. Holy Cow—Debra was on to something!

Self-talk is a key part of your identity. Neuroscience reveals that three key factors affect our sense of *identity*: 1) How we view ourselves; 2) how others view us; and 3) how we judge others or act toward others based on others' perception of us.[5] That first factor, how you view yourself, pops up in the form of self-talk. Self-talk is a natural, built in function of the brain.

There are two parts of the brain that are used for processing information relevant to the human identity. The first one is called the medial prefrontal cortex—I'll call this the "Medial part" (pardon my simple terms; that's how I roll). The Medial part has been called your "default mode." This is the part of your brain that's active when you're not focused on your external environment. I think of the Medial part as our "inner self-talk" part. The Medial part guides us to shift our thinking into egocentric mode—thinking all about ourselves. This is where self-talk happens.

The second part of the brain used for processing identity-related information is called the dorsal medial prefrontal cortex. I think of this as the "Dorsal part." The Dorsal part is activated when we're processing external, social information related to our position in a group, and others' perceptions of us. In plain English, this is where we're processing information about others in relation to our own identity.[6]

It's interesting that we process information about ourselves in a different part of the brain from where we process information about others. Even more interesting is the fact that the self-talk part of the brain (the Medial part) is our *default.* Our brains actually default to our egocentric mode. It's no wonder that self-talk has such a huge impact on our identities.

# 2

# The Right to Call Yourself a Victim (For a Minute)

**I think the greatest illusion we have is that denial protects us. It's actually the biggest distortion and lie. In fact, staying asleep is what's killing us.**

*Eve Ensler*

"Suck it up, Buttercup..." That's a phrase we jokingly use around the office and at home. I work with an amazingly talented team in my law firm. We all find a great deal of humor in the fact that ninety percent of the firm is comprised of women, and yet we all have robust amounts of testosterone in our systems. Not that there's anything at all wrong with having a sensitive spirit...but our team just doesn't cry easily or shy away from big challenges. I guess that's why we get along so well and truly feel like family to one another.

While we like to tease our co-workers to "suck it up," we know that when it comes to personal pain—offenses and wrongdoings suffered—sucking it up isn't the best motto for the average Buttercup.

Having lawyered for over 30 years now, I've defended and advocated for people who have truly experienced *victimization* by a wrongdoer—in one form or another. Consider:

- Julia, the stay-home mom whose husband was unfaithful. He ran up the family credit cards on a mistress while Julia gave up her career to raise four kids and support her husband's business dreams. Oh, and the really dirty (not-so-little) secret: He had a temper, and she had endured more than a dozen black eyes and split lips to prove it.

- Preston and Sally, the young-ish couple who sunk their life savings into their dream house only to discover their house had been illegally remodeled by the prior owner. Within six months of moving in, the house began creaking and popping...becoming so dangerous that Preston and Sally had to move out. Structural engineers determined the second floor was about to collapse into the first floor living room. On further inspection, construction experts discovered a Pandora's box of other defects. For example, the seller had wired parts of the home with extension cords buried in the walls instead of hiring an electrician, and used toothpaste in spots to grout the tile (among other crazy "short cuts").

- Mary, the widow who spent over 20 years building a successful nursing home business after the death of her husband. As she entered her elder years, she took on two business partners to help her operate the business, because Mary was slowing down and having some health problems herself. After 18 months of the new partnership, Mary discovered that the partners had embezzled most of the business' income and failed to pay the business' debts—leaving Mary personally liable for hundreds of thousands of dollars, and ultimately driving her into bankruptcy at the age of 73.

- Cheryl, whose step-father sexually assaulted her 10 to 15 times per month from age nine until she ran away at age 14. When Cheryl finally mustered the courage to tell her mother about the abuse, despite years of the stepfather's threats that if she told, he would kill her mother and her younger brother. Cheryl's mother was unable to accept the truth of what had happened and picked the abuser over Cheryl.

- Samuel, who paid a huge debt for his elderly father in order to save the father's house. The debt was for years of unpaid spousal support the father owed to Sam's now deceased mother. Sam's father had been physically abusive to Sam as a child and to Sam's mother, who divorced the father later in life. Soft-hearted Sam felt sorry for his father, because he was elderly and had cancer (but he was still mean, mean, mean). One of Samuel's brothers represented the dead mother's estate. The estate (brother) sued the father for the unpaid support (which would go to mom's heirs...the sons). Father was about to lose his house due to the debt. Father capitalized on Sam's kind spirit by promising to put Samuel on the deed to the father's house. He promised that Sam would get the father's house when the father died, if he paid off the debt to the mother's estate. Craving a relationship and his father's approval, Sam cashed out all of his retirement funds to pay his dad's debt. Despite Sam's extraordinary kindness, Sam's father reneged on his promise and changed his will to leave the house to Sam's brother—the very brother who was suing the father in the first place.

All these good people had one thing in common—they suffered great harm and enormous pain caused by others. These folks had every right to call themselves victims, because they, in fact, had been victimized.

**Striking Balance.** When people take on the victim persona for extended periods of time (even when they have great justification to do so) the persona easily lends itself to good old fashioned *wallowing*. Wallowing delays self-growth and healing. On the other hand denial, refusing to acknowledge when you've been victimized, can produce the same roadblocks to self-growth and healing as does the wallow-mode. *Wallowing* in the victim persona, and *denying* the fact that victimization has occurred, represent two polar extremes. While wallowing and denying are coping mechanisms and may be helpful for a short period of time, these responses can truly handicap us if we use either of them to permanently manage the pain of our circumstances.

Denial is the no-reaction reaction. Denial is pretending it didn't happen, or grossly minimizing what's happened. This is the classic "stuffing it" response; the ostrich head-buried-in-the-sand response to the internal conflict created by the bad event. What happens when you refuse to acknowledge that you've been victimized? The effects of the trauma fester like puss in an un-lanced boil (yes I know, this is an overtly gross mental picture I'm painting for you...but stay with me).

The analogy I'm about to share definitely tiptoes on the edge of "too much information" (or "TMI" as we like to say), but I'm going there anyway. So, as a kid I frequently experienced skin boils (I warned you...). My vivid memories of those episodes have stuck with me for life. If you've ever experienced a boil, then you know that they get bigger and more painful until they are cut open and drained. The cutting open part hurts for a few moments, and the draining part is just plain nasty. (If you've never seen a boil, search it on YouTube for an eye-opening, total gross-out experience.) But the cutting and draining are where the healing begins (and not before).

So it goes with the unacknowledged, unaddressed pain we experience after suffering harm. Stuff the pain and watch the puss spread beneath the surface. As the puss grows, the pain increases to maximum levels. Lance it and drain it. Acknowledge what happened, get it out of the system and watch the pain begin to subside, giving way to sweet relief.

Why is denial such an attractive response to suffering? Denial happens for a variety of reasons. Sometimes we deny ourselves *the right* to identify as a victim because we're thinking in the extreme. But let's be clear...you have *the right* to acknowledge what has happened to you when victimization occurs. The question is *how long* will you dwell in that house? I encourage you to be bold, step up with courage for a few moments, to call yourself "victim"...if only for a minute. Utter denial stops you from stepping onto the path of healing. Why is it an act of bravery to acknowledge what has happened to you? Because our culture has evolved into one of victim blaming and shaming.

**When "Victim" = Weakness.** Sometimes (okay, a lot of times) the word "victim" gets a bad rap. It's perceived as a weakness, something to hide. To many, the label "victim" is like a badge of humiliation, akin to the shaming narrative beautifully told in Nathaniel Hawthorne's classic *The Scarlett Letter*. The main character, Hester, had to wear a big red "A" (for adulterer) on her clothing after cheating on her husband and birthing a baby girl out of wedlock. The badge of humiliation was a life-long sentence for Hester, as long as she and her "illegitimate" daughter lived in Puritan 17th century Boston. The shame attached to Hester's identity drove her into an obsession where all she could think about was fleeing across the ocean to Europe, so no one would know of her past. Hester would do anything to detach from the shame of her identity.

When you associate what has happened to you with shame, guilt or weakness, hiding the victimization experience is a natural response. Are you minimizing what has happened to you? Have you taken time to thoughtfully examine the reason for the denial, the hiding? In working with people trying their best to ignore what has happened to them, my law office team and I often witness destructive behaviors and irrational emotional responses to seemingly benign situations. At least fifty percent of the time, these wounded clients have a negative association with the adjective "victim," and fear being perceived as weak or vulnerable.

A perfect example of the "victim" = weakness association is the man or boy who has suffered domestic violence or other abuse. Much of society views domestic violence as something that only happens to women and children. When a male is bullied, threatened, assaulted, stalked or abused by a female, a friend or an intimate partner, it's easily overlooked. Boys are repeatedly told "don't let 'em see you cry..." and other macho-man mantras. Add the cultural mores of "boys don't hit girls, no matter what," and we have a recipe for raising boys and men to suck it up and endure abuse in silence.

Well-meaning fathers and mothers groom their sons to believe that when assaulted, you better defend yourself...unless of course the attacker is a girl. So within the fabric of growing up male in America, a warped, devaluing belief is planted deep into the hearts of our boys and young men. It's that notion, that unspoken rule, that if you get hit or otherwise abused by a female, then it's time to just "man up." It's a notion permeating the day-to-day American experience. In church, we often hear that women and girls are the "weaker vessel." Boys often chide each other, "you're not going to let a *girl* beat you at this game, are you?" Young boys who cry because they are hurt or afraid get taunted by coaches, friends and siblings, "...don't be such a sissy" or "...stop acting like a girl." It's no wonder male victims of abuse associate personal weakness and shame with what has happened to them.

**The Pain-Bully Relationship.** Over the last 10 years, reported instances of bullying in America have risen to epidemic proportions. Maybe we just didn't hear about it before the flood of social media portals. But maybe it's something else.

Consider the "be strong, be brave, be victorious, slay the day..." rah, rah, rah messaging that is so prevalent these days (in fact, every day) on Facebook, Instagram and Twitter. Those messages are attractive. I love those messages for the most part, because they're inspiring. It's like having your own personal cheerleader. Then again, is there an unintended consequence to the unending streams of social media cheerleading?

In the midst of the social media deluge of "look at my perfect life" soundbites, have we developed an intolerance for public demonstrations of pain, fear and humiliation? Perhaps public demonstrations of pain and vulnerability just make us uncomfortable. Could it be that all our hero-worshipping, tough-as-nails, good-vibes-only focus has left us woefully unprepared to gaze into the face of real humanity, and do the hard work of loving others through true, raw pain?

What would happen to the bullying that goes on in our school yards and online if we taught our children that it's OK to feel bad, and we'll feel bad for them and *with them?* What if we became non-judgmental in the face of public displays of emotion? What if we stopped hating weakness and started embracing *all facets* of our humanity: The jubilant happy side, the neutral side, and the pain and suffering side? Is it possible that our population of home-grown bullies would decline?

A great deal of research is going on to find out what makes a person a bully. The findings are interesting: Bullying, at its core, is not about the person being bullied. Bullying is a *coping mechanism* used by the bully to deal with the stresses of trauma. Bullies are much more likely than the average person to have experienced a stressful event that has occurred in the prior five years. So like people who turn to alcohol to numb the pain, bullies turn to bullying (and sometimes violence) to cope.[7] It's no surprise that studies are showing that people who have been bullied themselves are twice as likely to bully someone else. It's an "I'll get them before they get me" mentality. What would happen if those bullies had stopped stuffing pain and confronted their feelings about the traumatic event they'd experienced?

Could it be that living in denial of victimization leads to bullying? An alarming number of bullies studied had stuffed their feelings of shame and humiliation at having been victimized. They felt powerless over their abusers, and they equated their shame and humiliation with weakness. The act of bullying provides an opportunity to focus attention on someone else and avoid negative attention directed at the bully. This is particularly true when the bully harbors low self-esteem and self-loathing. When confronted with others who appear vulnerable, bullies are able to distract themselves from their own pain by brutalizing others (more denial).

Denial of pain is a quiet poison. For the bully, perhaps the fuel that drives this epidemic would dry up if he or she had been allowed to be a shame-free "victim" for a short while, process the feelings and begin to heal.

**Victim Shaming and Blaming.** At its root, victim blaming happens when the victim is questioned about what *they—the victim—* could have or should have done differently to prevent what happened to them. Shaming occurs when the victim is ostracized for talking about the victimization, pursuing justice, bringing social awareness to the issue, and pursuing self-healing. Widespread victim blaming/

shaming makes us afraid and makes the denial response to trauma seem reasonable and safe. But *why* is victim blaming and shaming happening at all?

In the summer of 2016, Harvard University postdoctoral psychology associate Laura Niemi and Boston College psychology professor Liane Young published the results of their research on the victim blaming phenomenon.[8] Niemi and Young's research, which involved 994 participants and four separate studies, led to several significant findings, one of which is particularly relevant to this discussion. First, they noted that "moral values" play a large role in determining the likelihood that someone will engage in victim-blaming behaviors, such as rating the victim as "contaminated" rather than "injured," and thus stigmatizing that person more for having been the victim of a crime. Niemi and Young identified two primary sets of moral values: *Binding values* and *individualizing values*. While everyone has a mix of the two, people with stronger *binding values* tend to favor protecting a group or the interests of a team as a whole. Whereas people with stronger *individualizing values* are more focused on fairness and preventing harm to an individual.

Another prominent explanation for victim blaming/shaming is the "just world" hypothesis.[9] This is the idea that most of us want to see our world as just and fair, and that we have a strong *need* to believe that we all deserve what happens to us and the consequences that follow. The "just world" mindset is particularly prevalent in American culture. Many Americans are raised to believe that they can achieve the American Dream, and that they alone are responsible for their own destiny. I grew up in the well-known Southern California version of the Dutch Reformed Church of America, otherwise known as the Crystal Cathedral. Our pastor, Reverend Robert H. Schuller, regularly reminded the congregation, "...if it's going to be, it's up to me." Growing up in the seventies and eighties, "build your own destiny" was the common message in American culture.

When bad things happen to good people, the "just world" mindset drives unempathetic reactions to those victimized. Simply put, we are very uncomfortable with the notion that sometimes, bad things happen to the good guys. After all, if we accept the fact that really bad stuff sometimes happens to people who do all the "right" things...that means we must admit that we ourselves are susceptible to harm. Acceptance of reality bursts our bubble of security and control—until we learn to think of it differently.

Criminal defense attorneys engage in victim blaming all the time. To a great degree, it's part of their job. Defense attorneys use victim blaming as part of their defense cases, *because it works*. American rape victims are well-known examples of this. Take Sarah, a 20-something woman who spends an evening in a night club with friends, dancing and drinking into the wee hours of the night. She awakens in an unfamiliar hotel room, alone, battered and bruised. Later, it's determined that Sarah had passed out and her "friends," a group of college athletes from a prominent university, took her to their hotel room and raped her. Hotel security cameras captured the athletes dragging Sarah into the hotel room at 2:00 a.m., and it's not long before it's broadcasted across the evening news.

The defense attorney does his job. He points out to the jury that Sarah had been dressed provocatively (implying that she "asked for it"). He points out that Sarah and all the defendants voluntarily got drunk, insinuating that Sarah consented to group sex with the athletes. The defense's job is to plant reasonable doubt into the minds of the jury in order to get a not-guilty verdict. While these courtroom maneuvers are to be expected, what happens to Sarah in the court of public opinion? Those with strong *binding values* may be heard the loudest—blaming and shaming Sarah in order to protect the reputation of the beloved university and its high-profile athletic team. Those with a "just world" mindset may be tempted to jump on the blame/shame bandwagon, especially if they are parents of a young woman much like Sarah, or are young women themselves. The fact that such a horrible thing could have happened to Sarah is unnerving; after all, that means we are just as susceptible as Sarah.

**The Call to Courage—Emerge From the Shadows.** While the "just world" explanation of victim blaming and shaming makes a whole lot of sense, the key is to recognize that victim blaming is *not about you*. The phrase "hurting people hurt people" holds true, and I believe it's especially true of the victim blamers. Fear and uncertainty are the most common drivers of angry, ugly and unempathetic behaviors in modern culture. Despite the fear, and all the reasons denial might look like the safest response, I encourage you to resist the urge to go there. Staying in the shadows of denial is as counter-productive, if not more, than the habit of wallowing in a victim identity.

The polar opposite of the denial response is *wallowing* in the victim role. Wallowing is that thing we do for an extended period of time. Not for a valid moment or two. No, wallowing is about self-indulgence to the extreme, relishing and basking in the victim persona in order to get a pleasurable sensation—a pay-off. As we'll explore in the chapters that follow, wallowing in the victim role doesn't serve you (or others), but we can be tempted to do it because there are payoffs. But those payoffs are shallow, cheap thrills, if you will. As we'll see, wallowing in the shallows of a victim persona keeps us from the beautiful journey of self-growth and healing. In turn, we give our victimizers more of our power, while turning a blind eye to an opportunity-filled future.

As we proceed, I invite you to dance. This is a fine dance between souls who've been harmed, wronged, or suffered pain at the hands of another. Yet we dance together in a beautiful waltz of *balance*. On the edges of the dance floor are *wallow* and *denial*, two onlookers who've no interest in mastering the steps that create this exquisite, healing waltz.

# 3

# The Starting Point:
# Acknowledgment and Validation

**Trauma is personal. It does not disappear if it is not validated. When it is ignored or invalidated the silent screams continue, internally heard only by the one held captive. When someone enters the pain and hears the screams, healing can begin.**

*Danielle Bernock, Emerging with Wings:*
*A True Story of Lies, Pain, and the Love That Heals*

The healing process is halted unless we get on with the process of acknowledgment and validation. Acknowledgment means admitting or recognizing the fact that something not-so-great (OK, often something *really cruddy*) has happened. Acknowledgment is accepting the fact that *it happened*. This is the opposite of denial.

Validation is recognition of what you're feeling. Validating the feelings of pain. Validating the feelings of suffering, injustice. When we validate, we aren't judging whether our feelings are "right" or "wrong." We're not agreeing or disagreeing with the feelings. We are simply recognizing that we have the right to feel the way we do.

At the same time that you acknowledge and validate, remember who *you are....* You are not *what* has happened to you. You are not *defined by* your emotions. There is a difference between the acknowledging/validation task and your *identity.* As we launch into healing, the art of compartmentalizing comes into play. This can feel a bit schizophrenic at first, but it simply takes practice. With a neutralized perspective, and a little practice, you'll be able to compartmentalize and recognize the difference between acknowledgment/validation and who you really *are.*

**The Wall.** This starting place of acknowledgment and validation is not to be ignored. Really, you'll hit the proverbial wall and spend a whole lot of energy trying to avoid the issues that stubbornly resurface and never seem to go away. You'll find yourself in an unending game of emotional "whack-a-mole" (I always hated that game) until the starting place is found. If the pain and feelings from what happened are not allowed—not acknowledged—we set ourselves up for failure. In our rush to encourage each other to "get over it," we risk further shame and humiliation. After all, when I'm still "stuck" in my feelings of pain, anger, shame and not moving on right away, it's easy to conclude that there must be something wrong with me—that I must be weak compared to the rest of the world.

**Beachballs Under the Water.** I think most people have had ugly things happen in their lives and have tried to ignore the aftermath of the bad thing that happened. Sometimes we resent being inconvenienced by feelings of loss, sadness, hurt, anger, or vulnerability. We'd rather focus on the happy, but refusing to acknowledge and validate pain and feelings that require processing leads to unresolved "gunk." Unresolved gunk *always* shows up, somewhere down the road.

Over the years I have mediated *hundreds* of disputes. Watching people in all levels of conflict has been very instructive. For many, their response to conflict is denial or avoidance. Let's face it, the path of least resistance is to ignore conflict—at least it appears that way on the surface. However, when we are wronged, even victimized, denying or ignoring the conflict easily gives rise to *extreme* conflict. "Stuffing" what's happened to us is an attempt to gain instant *relief* from the anticipated pain and fear of confronting the negative experience. But that relief is short-lived, as the effects of the conflict continue to show up in various ways, no matter how hard we try to avoid or ignore it. I call this the "beachballs under the water" phenomenon.

Growing up in sunny Southern California, I spent the majority of my free time in the water—in the ocean, in swimming pools at friends' homes, in the local community or high school pools for swim team and water polo practice. We'd play for hours until we looked like prunes. We loved having those big, brightly colored beachballs in the water, and we'd compete to see who could hold the beachballs under the water the longest. With a beachball under the palm of each hand, we'd hold those balls down by our knees for a few seconds, sometimes even over a minute. But eventually our arms began to tire and shake, and those beachballs always popped up to the surface— no matter how hard we tried to keep them hidden under the water.

And so it is with internal pain, personal conflict, wounds suppressed and ignored. The healing remains stunted, halted. That is, until we embrace the fix: Embracing the pain and deciding to move through it. Deciding to go through it. Not around it or under it...but *through* it.

**Ready, Set, Go.** So where to start? Striking the balance between wallowing and denial isn't so hard to do once you understand two key things: First, we start healing from life challenges by acknowledgment and validation, through a "neutralized" lens. This "neutralizing" process means we acknowledge what has happened and validate our feelings about it and the consequences of what has happened factually. We don't allow the life challenge to "grow legs" and become bigger than it really is. This is where the words you use come into play, just like the example of my conversation with Coach Debra in Chapter One. You saw how I was "catastrophizing" to an extent as I described myself as "so overwhelmed." Catastrophizing is what psychology professionals call it when we irrationally believe a situation is far worse than it actually is. It's what we do when we're thoughtless and sloppy with our vocabulary and we throw around exaggeration adjectives like "overwhelmed," "disaster" or the like.

One of the most important tools I utilized as a mediator was the tool of "reframing." Each party to a dispute had their version of the facts. About three days before the mediation hearing each side would submit a mediation brief, presenting their side of the "story" to me. Each "story" was almost always infused with broad exaggerations of the impacts (damages) each side felt they were experiencing as a result of the conflict. I would move from the broad exaggerations to specifics—looking at the facts. In reframing the conflict, I would put together a neutral statement of a factual, specific timeline of what had happened and each party's claims. Then at the beginning of the mediation hearing, I would "reframe" the dispute and the order of the discussion in terms of the neutralized statement of the facts. This technique took the unproductive histrionics out of the discussion and made the problem feel much more "manageable" to everyone in the room. I took the wind out of the inflammatory sails, so to speak. So instead of stating, "...on June 1, 2010 Harold, a dirty dastard, cheated Maude out of her life savings and blew it all at the local casino," I'd reframe it with "on June 1, 2010 Harold used Maude's debit card to withdraw $5,000 from her bank account. On June 1, 2010 Harold spent $5,000 at the local casino."

This reframing process is extremely useful when we're dealing with our own personal approaches to pain. With acknowledgement and validation, neutralizing what has occurred helps us stay in the lane of balance and move along into healing. Remember the old saying, "Just the facts ma'am, just the facts."

The second key to striking the healing balance is *self*-acknowledgment and **self**-validation. One of the most productive things we can do in response to pain is to not expect acknowledgment or validation from *external sources*. To do so is to yield your self-determination and your power to someone or something else (but if someone else is kind enough to extend acknowledgment and validation, consider yourself blessed—that's icing on the cake).

As a woman of faith, I prefer to limit my reliance on external sources of acknowledgment and validation to my Creator. That's it. Sure, it's natural to seek comfort and understanding from those closest to us. But I'm talking about expectations here—other than yourself and your Creator, who else is really equipped to give you what you need? And why put your "hope" in others who are just fallible humans like you?

A common response to conflict by those wronged is the desire for an apology from the wrongdoer. What the wronged person is really wanting is acknowledgment and validation from the perpetrator. As a mediator, over the years I've helped write dozens of "apology" statements for parties in conflict (even though they have no legal significance) because it's what the wronged party felt they needed to get closure on the dispute. Here's the truth of the matter—none of those apologies were really necessary. Nine times out of ten, the person signing the apology was simply going through the motions to get the deal done, because it was demanded by the person wronged. The formal "apology" was typically viewed by the apologizer as a way to get a lawsuit dismissed.

These hollow apologies were so reminiscent of childhood, when I would be a rotten bully to my little sister and my mother would demand that I apologize. You know what that's like...angry child with arms crossed, teeth clenched, grudgingly uttering "...fine! I'm sorry" just to get the parental tongue-lashing over with. This is why the best form of acknowledgment begins within. The most important person to get an acknowledgment from, and validation of feelings from, is *you*. When we stop expecting acknowledgment and validation from others, we empower ourselves to start *healing*.

**Let's Start Now.** If these ideas are new to you, and you don't know where to start with self-acknowledgment and validation, let's start together. If no one has acknowledged what's happened to you, let this serve as my acknowledgment with you. What happened to you, happened. Remember, stick to the facts. Here are some examples:

"I was injured in a car accident."

"I've been diagnosed with cancer."

"My spouse and I are divorcing."

"I'm raising my children part of the time, and they're with my ex the other part of the time."

"I'm closing my business and starting a new job."

"I was in a physically abusive relationship."

Notice that we're not "acknowledging" exaggerations—stuff that's neither true, nor factual. No catastrophizing. Notice we're not acknowledging via statements like:

"My body was destroyed in a hit-and-run car crash."

"I'm a cancer victim."

"My husband left me and my life is over."

"I failed in business and am a bankrupted loser."

"I'm a battered spouse and a domestic violence victim."

We acknowledge what happened, but *you* are *not* what has happened to you.

Now for validation. Get quiet and think about how you've been feeling about what's happened. You are entitled to those feelings. They aren't right or wrong, they just *are*. It's OK—you be angry, sad, lonely, afraid, or whatever you feel. Your feelings are valid. Now tell yourself that—go ahead, say it: "I feel _____, and that's valid to have those feelings."

Congratulations—you've started the process of self-acknowledgment and self-validation.

# PART TWO

## THE VICTIM HABIT

--------------------------------

# 4

# How the Victim Habit Shows Up

**The mass of men lead lives of quiet desperation.
What is called resignation is called
confirmed desperation.
But it is a characteristic of wisdom
not to do desperate things.**

*Henry David Thoreau*

W e often think of habits as behaviors; things we "do." The word "habit" is typically associated with an undesirable act. We refer to "bad habits" as things we must "break" (notice the negative word association with habits—"bad," "break"). But habits, really, are just patterns—a series of behaviors. Not only are habits patterns of physical behaviors, but they also show up as patterns in the way we *think*.

Painful encounters, trauma and significant disappointments can easily trigger immediate mental stress. Thought patterns akin to an inner war can take over when our thoughts are touched by the pain, and we react. We talk to friends about it. We seek out medical solutions. We pursue sympathetic words from loved ones to comfort us.

We ruminate on the pain and begin to craft the narrative we tell ourselves about what happened to us. We formulate conclusions about ourselves in light of the trauma. And when the re-runs of the stories we tell ourselves become too much to bear, it's an easy leap into "solutions" that help shut down our thoughts, and numb the pain.

All these reactions to pain so easily become habitual thought patterns. Thought patterns are interesting because sometimes they allow us to live life on autopilot. Have you ever looked back on your week and thought, "Well that was a blur...where did the time go?" Or on Sunday evening—as you contemplate the upcoming week—have you ever thought, "Here we go, another week just like the rest..."? The tired saying "same sh@!, different day" is an outward manifestation of mental drifting. This mental drifting is really all about living in autopilot mode, living without intention, defaulting to thought patterns that keep us in neutral (not moving forward!).

Perhaps you respond to pain with the idea that a glass of wine helps you relax after a long day. Repeated to the point of *habit*, it becomes a tool to not only "relax," but to not think about things. That idea, when it becomes a pattern of thinking and doing on autopilot, easily turns into three or four glasses of wine a day.

In the lonely hours when the feelings of disappointment begin to bubble, you may pick up the phone or start texting a friend, expressing again the irritation of it all and gain the sympathetic ear. It's a conversation you can count on having with the loyal friend who is always willing to jump on the bandwagon of commiseration...commiseration without question, without disruption. This too, is mental drifting, a quiet form of unchallenged, unconscious living. When we live life on autopilot, in a state of unconscious living, those thought patterns quickly snowball into the Victim Habit.

The Victim Habit shows up in a myriad of ways. It's not a one-size-fits-all deal. Over the years, I've worked with a steady stream of clients who appear stuck, not growing nor advancing into exciting new seasons of their lives. While the result was the same (stuck in neutral, or sometimes in reverse), their Victim Habits varied. So how do we leave a Victim Habit behind, and put our lives into drive and hit the accelerator? By first understanding the different ways the Victim Habit shows up for us.

*Meet Lola, Queen of Victim Habits.* While there are many, I've identified six common Victim Habits below, though the list is most certainly not exhaustive. Before we dive in, let me first introduce you to Lola. Lola was unique in that she demonstrated not one, but all six of the Habits. Most people exhibit two or three, but Lola truly was a Victim Habit Hall of Famer. She was a sympathy-addict with a lot of Victim Habits that led her around by the nose.

My daughter Rachael is a young, up-and-coming divorce attorney. I've had the joy of getting to practice law with Rachael, mentoring her in the art of trial practice and counseling clients through matrimonial challenges. Rachael has a big heart, a sharp intellect and a massive drive to go to the mat in the face of injustice. These are all great strengths, but young lawyers frequently stub their toes early on in their careers as they learn how to *master* those strengths. That's exactly what happened to Rachael in her third year of law practice.

Part of mentoring is allowing the young attorney to learn which clients to take on and which clients to respectfully decline. Of course, you'll never develop that learned judgment without falling on your face a few times. Failure is a keen life coach if you embrace it. This learning process almost always involves taking that "case from hell" and dancing with that "client from hell." Nice terms, right? We've all been there, no matter the profession, and Rachael was no exception. One of Rachael's first solo consultations was an encounter with Lola. In hindsight, Lola threw down a lot of red flags, indicators that she *was not* the client for us.

Because we handle family law cases, we have a strict policy against clients bringing their children to the law office. We believe that when mommy and daddy are splitting up, children should never experience going into lawyers' offices or hearing bad things about their parents. These are memories kids should never have. So, we advise clients that they are not—under any circumstances—to bring their children to our office. We believe this so firmly that a potential new client calling for a consultation is told about our "no kids" policy on the phone, and reminded in several follow-up emails before their appointment.

So what did Lola do when she came in for her initial consultation with Rachael? You guessed it. She brought her seven-year-old daughter with her, and our loving team members accommodated them. After all, Lola's was the last appointment of the day and she had an "emergency" court hearing coming up in just a few days. (Another attorney red flag; clients who wait until the 11th hour to deal with a court hearing.)

Lola told quite a story. Her husband was a raging alcoholic and severely abusive. He beat Lola in front of the child and kicked the dog. Lola had managed to get a temporary restraining order on her own, and now a court hearing was coming up to address Lola's request for a permanent restraining order. Lola explained that she was so distraught she couldn't work, so she went on disability. Lola claimed that she and her daughter were about to be out on the street because the husband had cut them off financially. Lola felt she had to hide in the homes of friends, even though the husband had been removed from the family home under the restraining order. Rachael's inner justice-warrior was piqued.

But here's the thing: What was scheduled as a 90-minute consultation turned into a three hour gab-fest. Lola just wouldn't stop talking. The more she talked about her victimization, the more invigorated she seemed to become, and she talked faster and faster with renewed energy. Rachael was having a hard time corralling the conversation and bringing it to a close. Lola's daughter was down the hall in a small conference room, enjoying snacks and coloring books provided by our compassionate law staff. But Lola's daughter grew antsy as time went on, and she began running through the lobby trying to amuse herself. Of course, that turned our staff into babysitters. Despite the child's multiple interruptions, Lola kept yammering on and on, seemingly unaware of time and her child's understandable intolerance for a three-hour coloring-book session.

Around 7:00 p.m. Rachael finally made her way into my office where I was wrapping up for the night. She told me about poor Lola. I pointed out the multiple red flags the team had observed. But the young justice-warrior was riled up, and she was certain she could really help this lady. I left the decision to Rachael, and authorized her to accept Lola's case if she so chose.

What followed was four months of wrangling with Lola. As Rachael began to forge a path for Lola to get out of pain and into a new life where things go well and Lola could start to feel good about her home life and get back to work, Lola freaked. I mean a total, utterly irrational freak out. Lola just wasn't having it. She was not willing to let go of her Victim Habits.

Shortly after taking the case, Rachael had several revelations. She discovered that Lola wasn't in financial dire straits after all. Lola had failed to tell Rachael that she'd inherited close to a quarter million dollars ($250,000) and had that money stashed in a bank account. It's no surprise that Lola didn't tell Rachael about the inheritance money; that information simply didn't support Lola's adopted victim identity.

As the case progressed, Lola refused to move back into her family home (even though the husband was staying far away in light of the restraining order). Instead, Lola took her daughter out of school and moved several towns away, into a *homeless shelter*. What?! With $250,000 in the bank? Living in a homeless shelter *supported* Lola's Victim Habits.

But the facts kept getting in Lola's way. When they went to court for the permanent restraining order, the husband had *also* filed a request for a restraining order. Witnesses and documented evidence showed up with him, supporting the husband's claim that Lola had physically assaulted him. The reality was, *both* Lola and her husband had become physically abusive with each other.

Despite the dishonesty and bad facts, in the end Rachael was able to negotiate a complete settlement of the case, including a healthy amount of child and spousal support and the reimbursement of a large portion of Lola's legal fees from the husband. Rachael got Lola a *phenomenal result* because she's a hugely talented lawyer and an ace negotiator (proud mama, chest thump here). The negotiated agreement got Lola 10 times more than she would have *ever* received had the judge decided. And yet, Lola was unhappy. In fact, she wanted to unwind the settlement the day after it was signed and entered by the judge.

What was going on? Lola couldn't stand that the conflict and all the attention she got from it was over. Instead of being willing to feel good, Lola turned on Rachael. She accused her of all kinds of horrible things, when most clients in the same situation would have been singing Rachael's praises. What the heck was wrong with Lola? *The answer is simple:* Lola was butting up against her Victim Habits. Resolving the drama of the legal case was like taking crack away from an addict, cold turkey, and Lola turned angry and ugly.

**Victim Habit #1: The Cheap Thrill of Attention.** Attention was at the center of Lola's existence. Much of Lola's irrational, ugly behavior was in reaction to the loss of the attention she so relished. Lola's drama-filled life was the supply of that attention. Lola just wasn't willing to have things go well in her life because the cheap thrill of attention would be gone.

When bad things happen to us, compassionate people often feel sorry for us. And let's be honest…it feels good (most of the time) when caring people are willing to listen to our story and validate our pain. Those same caring people are often inspired to do something nice for us (especially the empaths), and that feels nice. But in the long run, others feeling sorry for you—or even *you* feeling sorry for you—doesn't truly serve you.

Have you ever known someone who has little to no long-term relationships, yet is eager to tell their story to anyone who'll listen? This is the person people start avoiding at church, work, or social events because the storytelling is nonstop. It's smothering and it's a time suck ("…tick-tock, tick-tock, when is this lady gonna stop talking…?" you think to yourself). This is the person who goes through a series of doctors, rehashing their story and seeking a physician who exudes more sympathy than the last. Sometimes we see the sympathy-addict going to extremes to stay in character.

A steady focus on garnering sympathy from others is a game of sabotage; of getting in your own way. Lola's story is a perfect example of that game. Sure, there's the feel-good moment when someone feels our pain, and sometimes they do nice things for us in an effort to "help" us in our moment of crisis. But staying in this zone is like a sugar rush. It becomes addicting and makes us fat and unhealthy. It's a cheap thrill that doesn't serve us.

The cheap thrill of attention can become quite a convenient smokescreen. It promotes internal excuses for not getting serious about cultivating *joy* in your life. Learning to consistently feel good and have things go well in your life is a threat to drama-driven attention. Drama is a never-ending source of hollow attention, and the call for sympathy.

Prolonged sympathy and external attention over things that happened to you in the past are traps. This Victim Habit lies to us. It tells us that it's *not possible* to consistently experience joy-filled living without the newfound attention from others. After all, when I'm a victim of my circumstances and garner attention as a result, it's easy to suddenly feel *significant* where I otherwise may not. Chasing significance in this way is a seduction presented by the Victim Habit. This becomes a "forest for the trees" issue, where we fear disrupting this Victim Habit in light of the immediate, temporary comfort we'll forego to do it.

**Victim Habit #2: Self-Imposed Helplessness.** This is the Habit of focusing on all the reasons "why not" when presented with the path forward. Our hall-of-famer, Lola, presented heavily in this area. The "no-kids-at-the-law-office" policy didn't apply to Lola, because after all (she justified), hers was the last appointment of the day. After all, Lola had an "emergency" court hearing a few days away…and she just couldn't get a babysitter. Lola also couldn't work because she was too distraught, couldn't stay in her home out of fear, and couldn't rent an apartment because she just couldn't "afford it" (except for that $250,000 in the bank; but don't let the facts get in the way of a good Habit). On and on it went.

It's so easy for our brains to immediately call out all the possible hurdles to a new plan of action. Helplessness is comfortable, because it allows us to avoid disruption to our adapted circumstances. For Lola, her self-imposed helplessness also kept her in attention-getting mode. Helplessness was comfortable because it gave Lola an excuse to not take *action*.

When hurdles, helplessness, and other limiting beliefs are challenged, inertia shows up. Inertia can feel like a hundred foot high-and-wide speed bump that cannot be gone around. It's that little devil you experience when shifting from stagnancy to *forward movement*. You'll continue to linger in a state of rest (or comfortable dysfunction) until the inertia is changed by something *external*. Depending on the meaning you give to forward movement, it can be tiring to think about disrupting inertia. In the moment, you may think it's easier to sink back into the known, into the "comfort" of the victim role, and therefore change nothing.

Shifting from a stagnant, motionless state to one of action requires energy. I experience a subtle push-back against the shift every time I head out to surf. I get to the beach, unpack my stuff, pull my board off the SUV, wiggle into my wetsuit and head down to the water. I stand there for a few moments looking for a channel to paddle through, out to the lineup. Sometimes I wait for a set to blow through (to avoid jumping into a washing machine situation; doing cartwheels under the water isn't all it's cracked up to be). When it's time to throw the board into the water and head out, here comes my 60 seconds of hesitation. I'm comfortable standing there in the sand in my dry wetsuit, warm and relaxed, until I tell myself "...come on, let's get this show on the road!" The show gets on the road (or in the waves) when I exert a burst of energy and jump on in. Welcome to the inertia war.

**Victim Habit #3: Playing Small.** This Habit runs an excuse factory. The factory's mission is to protect you from all the perceived risks of chasing your dreams and stepping into your higher potential. Playing small was exactly what Lola was doing when she tried to back out of the plum deal her attorney got her. Instead of stepping into her potential of a calm, financially secure and violence-free life, Lola began chasing the short-term comfort of playing small. For Lola, staying in the space of relational and legal drama was safe. It gave her the excuse she needed to not rejoin the workforce. She used her small place to avoid becoming a *giver* in this world rather than constantly taking from it. By playing small, Lola turned a blind eye to the next big thing standing just beyond her fear.

The Playing Small Habit means you accept fear-based excuses for not leaning into your great big potential. After all, what if you lean in and don't achieve what you've set out to do? This is all about *fear:*

- Fear of commitment.
- Fear of failure.
- Fear of making irreparable mistakes.
- Fear of outshining others.
- Fear of criticism.
- Fear of uncertainty.
- Fear of risk.

What's interesting, though, is that failure is a *key element* of success. There truly are no "overnight" success stories. Scratch the surface of those who've climbed the ladder to success and you'll find that the steps to the top were a series of tests and failures, laced with shots of fear. Each rung on that ladder was reached through conscious recalibration. Test, fail, recalibrate, advance. Failures are what catapult us, unless we drink the Kool-Aid they offer, and believe the lie that the Playing Small Habit leads to a safe, fulfilling life.

**Victim Habit #4: Get Them, Before They Get You**. A seemingly logical response to trauma is to wall off emotionally and relationally. It's tempting to avoid vulnerability and exposure to being hurt again. Many people go so far with the vulnerability avoidance that they turn into relational porcupines. They become prickly, stand-offish and are prone to lash out at people. This is the "I'll get you, before you get me" Habit.

It's understandable to want to pull into a hard, protective shell—like a turtle—and protect yourself from further harm. Lola was very much like this, and after lots of practice she turned into a bully. The Get Them, Before They Get You Habit results in ugly behavior toward people who love you and want to help you. This Habit destroys relationships and opportunities, because deep, quality relationships will in fact expose you to getting hurt on some emotional level. It's the nature of the beast. Opportunities to grow and expand come with risk; risk of failing, of trying something new and unknown, and maybe making some mistakes along the way. In an effort to avoid getting hurt again at all costs, you destroy relationships before they get too serious, and destroy new opportunities before it's time to perform.

Victimization, left unprocessed, can leave you feeling like you're not *enough*. Like you deserved what happened to you, because you're not loveable enough, not smart enough, not pretty enough, not talented enough, and not worthy of good things. These feelings of inadequacy feed insecurity, creating a white-knuckle approach to life where we hold on tight. So tight that we try to control everyone and everything around us. What drives that? Fear that if we don't control and micromanage others, they won't *voluntarily* stay in relationship with us. After all, if I'm truly not *enough*, why would they stay and love me if they aren't required to? Welcome to the great lie generated by fear.

This was Lola. She had a small group of friends and family show up to court to support her, after she rallied the small army through pleading and demanding. But Lola turned on them and her attorney, Rachael, when they counseled her to the path of resolution and elimination of the drama. They invited Lola to imagine how happy life could be if she put the conflict behind her and focused on healing. Lola got aggressive and verbally abusive. She was going to get everyone before the perceived risk of a new life got her.

**Victim Habit #5: The Blame Game.** The Blame Game Habit is all about refusing to take ownership of your life, your choices and the consequences of your choices. This is the free pass mindset, where the bad crud that's happened to you is the justification for not owning your choices. After all, you can't do or be _____ (fill in the blank) because _____ (fill in the blank some more) has happened to you, and people just don't understand.

For Lola, she had no income and was unhappy that the judge would not award her as much spousal support as she demanded. Seeing no evidence that Lola was medically unable to work (as she claimed), the judge indicated that spousal support would be lower because she should be working full-time. Lola was outraged. She moved into a homeless shelter with her child to try to prove a point to the judge. After all, Lola reasoned, she couldn't be expected to work when her ex-husband had been so abusive. (Forget about the abuse she dished back at him.) Because Lola was caught up in the Blame Game Habit, it then became both the judge's fault *and* her ex-husband's fault that she was "out on the street" with no money. (Don't let that quarter of a million in her bank account get in the way of a good argument....)

**Victim Habit #6: Can't Say No (Boundaries).** This Habit is quite the opposite of the blame game. When you feel bad about yourself and begin to wonder if maybe you "deserved" what happened to you, a boundary problem often develops. This is really a people-pleasing habit. In a desire for love and acceptance, you say "yes" to everything.

Jillian was caught up in this habit, big time. A well-known hospital consultant in the community, Jillian was active in many non-profit organizations and served on their boards. She quickly became known as the "go-to" lady when it came to free consulting services for good causes, because Jillian never said "no." But Jillian had a secret;

a surprising and sad back-story. At home, Jillian's husband was violent. He was an immigrant from South America, having grown up in a patriarchal, male dominant culture. Jillian's husband had been physically abusing her behind closed doors *for years*. No one in the community would have guessed, because Jillian was a well-educated professional, seemingly confident and polished. She hid it well.

Over time, Jillian's people-pleasing ways became a huge hurdle. She was overcommitted *all the time*. This left Jillian very little time to do the work that paid the bills. Her business suffered and before she knew it, Jillian was in high conflict in both her home life and in the consulting business she once loved. A victim of domestic violence, Jillian soldiered on in the Can't Say No Habit until she broke...literally. Broken at home and at work, Jillian's business failed and she had no alternative but to declare bankruptcy.

In a strange way, our gal Lola was knee deep into this Can't Say No Habit as well. It showed up in her relationship with her seven-year-old daughter. If little Suzie-Q didn't want to go to school on a particular day, Lola gave in and would take her to a theme park or take her shopping. Great way to use child support money, right? Lola had convinced herself that Suzie-Q deserved to have a "break" from the norms of school life and childhood disciplines, because she had grown up in a "battle zone" (as Lola described it). I'm sure you're not surprised to know that Suzie-Q started becoming quite entitled, and "spoiled brat" became a good description for Suzie-Q's behavior in light of Lola's unbridled indulgence of her child's whims.

You are not a horrible, failure of a person if you've gotten into some of the Victim Habits above (or others not described here). The good news is, *you're identifying them!* Acknowledging the habit is the first step to getting out of it. Habits aren't dissolved over night, but they are *replaceable*. Now that you've taken a look at the habit you're in you can begin to take action to cultivate a *new and better habit*. There's hope! Keep reading.

# 5

## Good Grief and the Masquerade Bawl

**There is a time for everything, and a season for every activity under the heavens...a time to weep and a time to laugh, a time to mourn and a time to dance.**

*Ecclesiastes 3:1, 4*

Before we look at why operating within Victim Habits hinders you from living your best life—and before we address practical ways to pull out of Victim Habits—it's important to make a big fat distinction here: A Victim Habit is *not* the same as grief or depression. *Do not confuse grief or depression for a Victim Habit.* I recognize this can be dangerous territory. I know what I'm not (i.e., I'm *not* a therapist or any kind of medical or health care professional), so I certainly do not want to get out of my lane here. Please, please, please do not jump to the conclusion that you or a loved one is simply in a Victim Habit if there's a real possibility that extended grief or depression are in the mix. Depression is typically described as an intense, continuing sadness rooted in a chemical imbalance in the brain. Extended grief is acute, experienced over a long duration.

Grieving is critical to moving through trauma. I cannot express this enough...*grieving is necessary!* Let us not confuse wallowing and denial (foundational elements of Victim Habits) with grieving. Grief is a God-given *gift*. It's the balm to our raw, wounded souls. The necessary antidote to loss. And without grief, we risk living in a tragic melodrama, on a seemingly unending video loop. Post-traumatic life without grief robs us of *hope.*

And while there's a distinction between grief and Victim Habits, there's also a connection between the two. What does grief have to do with victimization? Plenty. Grief happens when we experience the loss of something important to us. Most of us associate grief with the loss of a loved one, but really, it's about loss in general. If you think about it, life challenges, traumas, and victimization frequently involve the loss of something important in our lives. For the rape victim it may be the loss of physical health, loss of trust in dating partners, loss of confidence and loss of feelings of dignity. For the 62-year-old gentleman whose 401k tanked in a down economy, it may be the loss of economic security, the loss of freedom to retire and travel the world with his wife. For the child of sexual abuse, it's the loss of innocence, societal acceptance, and self-worth.

**Grief Typologies.** Grief studies have come a long way in the last 25 years. In psychological circles, "types" of grief have emerged such as "normal grief" and "complicated grief." According to the famed Mayo Clinic in Rochester, Minnesota, "normal" grief is a period of sorrow, guilt, anger and numb feelings that gradually ease over time. Under "normal" grief, you're eventually able to accept the loss and move forward in life. Then there's "complicated grief." This is where painful feelings last so long and are so severe that you have trouble with recovery, acceptance and resuming normal life routines. Medical experts diagnose patients with "complicated grief" occurring when the patient is unable to move through the general "stages" of grief within a year. "General stages" of grief have been described as denial, anger, bargaining, depression, and acceptance. I don't necessarily buy the year thing because some factors just take more time to process. Symptoms of complicated grief have been described as detachment from others, bitterness, lack of trust in others, belief that you are at fault or to blame for the trauma, hyper-focus on the trauma, and inability to enjoy life or reflect on positive experiences.[10]

**Ignore the Grief Process and You'll Embrace the Victim Habit.** Grieving and developing Victim Habits go hand in hand. Habits aren't things we "fall into." To the contrary, habits are patterns developed over time, built on repeated behaviors. While there is no "right way" to grieve, grief is one of those things that if ignored, becomes another beach ball under the water. Could it be that failure to grieve (or failure to *productively grieve*) gives way to the dreaded Victim Habit? I argue yes...rather, HECK yes.

Grief is a process that we *move through*. The habitual "victim" does quite the opposite. He or she makes a choice to languish in a negative place. To receive the payoff of the Victim Habit. Operating within the Victim Habit is like permanently camping at a rest stop. It's a place meant to be visited for a brief time; not a place designed for permanent residency. On the other hand, grief is something we choose to acknowledge, to accept, *to do.*

Famed writer and deep thinker C.S. Lewis (author of *The Chronicles of Narnia*) married late in life. As the last of his Narnian books were being published, Lewis married his longtime friend, Joy Davidman Gresham, in a civil ceremony. They married not for love, but for the sole purpose of allowing Joy to remain in Britain. You see, Joy was previously married, had two children and lived in America when her then-husband decided to divorce her, in order to marry his mistress. Joy was British, but in order to be able to return "home" permanently, she needed to be married to a Brit. Enter longtime friend "Jack" (C.S. Lewis). And so it was, in 1956, that the two old friends married out of convenience. A "favor" to Joy, if you will.

Shortly after Jack and Joy married, they learned that she had terminal cancer. Yet through it all, the relationship between Joy and Jack deepened and a great love of their lives developed. Months later in December 1956, Jack and Joy Lewis married *again,* this time in a Christian ceremony at Joy's bedside in the hospital. Remarkably, Joy's cancer went into remission and for the next two years Joy was able to move home with Jack, and even travel. Their love and joy deepened. Tragically, in 1960 Joy's cancer reappeared and she died at the age of 45 in July of 1960. C.S. Lewis went into a deep, inconsolable period of bereavement. Today it would likely be diagnosed as complicated grief.

The love story of C.S. Lewis and his beloved Joy was told beautifully in Sir Richard Attenborough's acclaimed film, *Shadowlands.* Yet, in the aftermath of Lewis' tragic loss, a keen revelation came to him. A significant tool for Lewis' extended bereavement was, of course, his writing. He poured out his soul, expressing with great intensity his sorrow in a journal. That grief journal was later published as a collection in 1961 called, "A Grief Observed". Lewis published the book under the pen name N.W. Clerk. (It's rumored that in an ironic twist, a number of concerned friends sent Lewis a copy of *A Grief Observed* noting they thought it might help him, not knowing it was Lewis' own work.)

C.S. Lewis shared his new-found revelation in *A Grief Observed*— that grief was not a state of mind, but in fact, a journey forward:

*"I thought I could describe a state; make a map of sorrow. Sorrow, however, turns out to be not a state but a process. It needs not a map but a history, and if I don't stop writing that history at some quite arbitrary point, there's no reason why I should ever stop."*[11]

Lewis discovered that his grief was not only a process, but also a cognizant choice that was his to make. Lewis' sorrow was a history that he had furiously journaled about, in a great catharsis, no doubt. But as he noted, he had the power to stop writing "that history" at a point he chose, lest he never move on with his life.

Like C.S. Lewis, modern-day Pastor Rick Warren of Saddleback Church in Lake Forest, California, also argues that grief is a *choice*. Pastor Rick and his wife Kay suffered an unimaginable season of pain when in 2013, their youngest son Matthew took his own life at the age of 27. Matthew had suffered for years with severe depression and mental illness. Rick and Kay Warren spoke publicly and transparently about their loss and the grieving process. Pastor Rick encourages us to be intentional about our grief, and to recognize that grief is a *tool* to manage life transitions. Arguing that grief is a *choice* and is *necessary*, Pastor Warren noted:

> *The bad things that happen to you are not your choice. But grief is a choice. You may say, "I don't like feeling sad." Not everything that's helpful and healthy feels good. You've got to let yourself mourn losses so that you can move on with your life and receive God's blessing.[12]*

Choosing not to grieve shows up in the form of Victim Habits. Instead of grieving, we may seek attention and sympathy at every turn. Instead of mourning our losses, we may feign helplessness in order to avoid the work of moving through grief. Instead of grieving, we may play small and safe or lash out at others before things get risky and cause the discomfort of growth. Rather than move into and through our sorrow, we may get busy blaming others instead of taking ownership of our choices and the resulting state of affairs. Choosing to avoid grief, we may keep ourselves busy by saying "yes" to everything in order to avoid the quiet, contemplative moments of sitting with our pain and sorrow long enough to truly *mourn*.

All of these avoidance tactics are nothing more than a masquerade. The grief remains, no matter how hard you try to mask it. The behaviors attendant with the Victim Habits are a different kind of bawling. Yes, a grand "masquerade bawl," if you will. But as Pastor Rick Warren so honestly pointed out, grieving is helpful and healthy, yet it doesn't feel good most of the time. Beyond the grief, however, your Creator offers you *life* and blessings beyond your imagination. If you've been holding back, now is your time. Embrace good grief so you may move forward into all that goodness awaiting you.

# 6

# The Price of Poker
# (Why a Victim Identity Doesn't
# Serve You Long-Term)

**As my sufferings mounted I soon realized that
there were two ways in which I could respond to
my situation—either to react with bitterness or seek
to transform the suffering into a creative force.
I decided to follow the latter course.**

*Dr. Martin Luther King, Jr.*

When you adopt Victim Habits and remain in those patterns, it's easy for the victim identity to take over. In the midst of life challenges, we naturally question who we are. We're vulnerable to negative redefinitions of our identity. Living in the Habits is like pouring gallons of water onto a dry sponge of identity. You begin to adopt the label "victim" as your conscious identity. But that identity is not truly sustainable over time when your goal is to live to your fullest potential, experience joy again, and engage in fulfilling relationships.

So why is a victim identity so darned comfortable? If the victim identity is unsustainable, why does it seem attractive, at least to our unconscious mind? Because there's a payoff. We don't continue to behave in patterns where there is no payoff. The other side of the payoff coin is the price; the cost. For every action there is a consequence and the victim identity comes with a hefty price tag.

**The Case for Rejecting a Victim Identity.** The victim role, played out long-term, delivers significant consequences. In the Bible, the devil is described as a "thief in the night," and I think of a victim identity in the same vein. It truly is a thief in the night, because it operates under a veil of darkness; it's sneaky and strikes when we're not conscious of it. What does this thief rob us of?

*Power.* One of the most thrilling characteristics of the human condition, in my opinion, is that we have *choices*. From the moment your eyelids pop open each morning to the moment you drift off into a deep sleep each night, you make hundreds of choices. The net results in our lives are the sum of the hundreds of daily choices we make. With the victim identity, the choices made there—within the Victim Habits—are extremely disempowering. The choices made within the Habits are limiting. Taking the common Victim Habits we've already identified, here are examples of the power-sucking consequences related to the choices made within each Habit:

- *Cheap Thrill of Attention.* Choosing behaviors that garner immediate attention means we make a trade-off. Instead of investing time and energy into the needs of others, we suck the energy out of relationships to feed the attention addiction. This creates a one-way relationship. Relationships have "gas tanks." The needs of one person deplete the gas tank, and unless that tank is replenished it runs out of gas, and the needs of the other person go unmet. You can only run on empty for so long before the unilateral relationship is abandoned. The choices made in the Cheap Thrill of Attention Habit limit your ability to have deep, nourishing, long-lasting relationships, and that's a huge power-suck.

- *Self-Imposed Helplessness.* I strongly believe that choosing helplessness is a significant relinquishment of power. I've seen this over and over in my 30+ years of practicing law and leading people. There isn't a single incident in all the disputes I've handled—and people I've helped—where self-imposed helplessness has led to long-term empowerment. The thief pops out, large as life, under this Habit. At first glance, living in self-imposed helplessness feels like you're in a position of power. After all, when you're "helpless" many people will initially come to the rescue. That feels powerful. The reality is, you are *giving away* your power by living within the confines of big limitations. When you are helpless, you are dependent. When you are dependent on others, the power has been handed over. This is not to say that we should never depend on others. We need people. We're better in community with others, but we should never play helpless where we in fact *can choose* to help ourselves. There is power in the choice.

- *Playing Small.* Like self-imposed helplessness, playing small is a choice to limit your potential and your gains. Limit your potential and you limit your power. Shortly after I was elected to public office as a city councilwoman and a mayor, it became clear to me that the position conferred *influence* upon me. I didn't see myself as "powerful," yet members of the community—real estate developers, business owners and other governmental employees—did. They saw that council role as having a great deal more influence than I realized. Influence is powerful but more than that, it's a huge responsibility, in my book. When you play small, you limit your influence (and increased responsibilities). In dodging responsibility and influence, you also limit your pay-offs. Just like the financial investment game, the higher the risk the larger the payoff.

- *Get Them Before They Get You.* The power-rob here seems so obvious. Seriously, when we play the aggressor and actively destroy our relationships before they get too deep, we are choosing to play in the shallows. Most people go into relationships truly wanting to know and be known. To love and be (unconditionally) loved. To go deep. People are seeking that soul mate...the ultimate in intimacy and bondedness. The choice to sabotage a relationship as it moves into the deep commitment, risk-laden true intimacy stage robs you of the power of the deep-rooted, "in it to win it" friendships, marriages, partnerships, and life-bonds. There is *power* in healthy, deep-rooted human connection. When you have strong, healthy people in your inner circles, you are empowered and emboldened to take on the next big thing. The "Get Them Before They Get You" Habit blows up the relational support systems and runs off with your power. Damn thief.

- *Blame Game.* Blaming others for the consequences of your own crappy decisions is the quintessential example of non-accountability. (I know what you're thinking... "yeah, thanks Captain Obvious...like you needed to point that out."). While this seems obvious, people still ride the blame train all day long. Why is the shift to taking full ownership of our choices empowering? Because in the owning, comes the practice of doing the higher-level work to gain the higher-level payoffs. There are no long-term, successful leaders who lack personal accountability. The buck stops with them. Why? No one will follow a "leader" who doesn't take ownership of the choices they make, because that's not inspiring leadership. Blame-shifting means lack of credibility. No one will trust you or work with you if you are in the habit of blaming everyone else for your own stuff. Where the blame game is played, the players lose a vast array of opportunities for *growth*. It is in the errors and deep consideration of the mistakes where growth happens—and that's powerful. No accountability = no power.

- *Can't Say No (Boundaries).* Letting external forces dictate your every day choices robs you of the power to advance your mission, your calling, *your* purpose for being on this planet. Have you ever started your day with one or two things you intended to do, but got sidelined by interruptions and distractions? Those days are frustrating, and usually happen when we allow external forces and demands to take priority over the one or two really important tasks we set out to accomplish. The result is the unimportant things (interruptions and distractions) get the attention while the truly important things don't get done. So it is with the lack of boundaries inherent in the Can't-Say-No Habit. You give your power away (or it feels like it slips away, like sand through the hourglass). There is great power in the "no."

**Long Term Well-Being.** Adopting the victim identity not only steals your power; it robs you of joy, groundedness and overall well-being. It promotes a perpetual state of suffering. This suffering shows up physically, psychologically or spiritually (or any combination of the three). Here's what it may look like:

- *Physical Suffering.* The constant rehashing of life challenges can keep the physical stress of the trauma going. Stress regularly shows up in our physicality. Years ago when I was running my law firm while simultaneously serving as the Mayor of a city of 110,000 people, I had what appeared to be a heart attack. After being rushed to the hospital and undergoing a zillion tests (and one week of laying around a hospital room... scream!) it was determined that I had suffered an acute stress attack. The external stressors I was under manifested themselves in physical reactions in my body. Stress is a real deal and it can make you truly sick. I can only imagine what it's like to have a significant life challenge and mentally rehash it over and over again. Your blood pressure is sure to rise, and the physical body reacts. Then there are the Victim Habits that facilitate non-accountability. The Habits tend to excuse poor eating, lack of exercise, and refusal of medical attention. Before you know it, the "victim" looking back at you in the mirror is unrecognizably unkempt, has gained 75 pounds and is in very poor health.

- *Psychological Suffering.* The Habits are a mind trip, for sure. With the habitual attention seeker, the support system goes away and she's left alienated and alone. With the self-induced helpless victim, becoming overly dependent on others leads to self-doubt and lack of confidence, which can increase fear and anxiety of being alone. Psychologically speaking, the habit of helplessness also leads to lazy thinking, where the victim gets out of the practice of thinking through challenges, making decisions to act, and then executing. This is anxiety and depression in the making. The same goes for the other Victim Habits. There are always negative psychological consequences that inevitably lead to suffering.

- *Spiritual Suffering.* The Habits all have one thing in common: They support a life of non-faith. Faith is having the confidence that what we hope for is going to happen, and being certain of things we don't yet see.[13] This involves believing and trusting in the Divine; trusting that your Higher Power is ultimately in control and is working through your life challenges for your good and your growth. The Habits drive a wedge between you and a vibrant spiritual life. Spirituality (connecting with God or whatever you care to call your Creator) is disrupted by the Victim Habits, because the Habits perpetuate busyness and chaos. The Habits advocate for trying all manner of action to fill the void that a dynamic spiritual life fulfills.

When you passionately seek attention and sympathy, your eyes are on yourself instead of God and on helping others. When you engage in self-imposed helplessness, you reject God's invitation to step out in faith and grow in physical and psychological strength. When you play small and safe, you stunt personal and professional growth, passing up opportunities the Universe has seen fit to offer you. When you engage in relational sabotage and control, keeping friends and loved ones at arms' length distances, you foreclose on the ability to enjoy intimacy with others and in communion with God. When you refuse to acknowledge your own mistakes, weaknesses, or contributions to your problems, you refuse the necessary discomfort God allows us to experience when She stretches our faith to improve our character. Finally, when you lack boundaries and say yes to everything in order to please everyone, you lose sight of the primary purposes you were made for, and the primary mission you were sent here to accomplish.

Taking time to be still and humble before God, and following the promptings of your Creator, takes faith. It takes courage too, because in so doing, you are allowing the hard work of healing, honest self-reflection and working through pain to occur. As the scripture comfortingly says, "...draw near to God, and He will draw near to you."[14] God hasn't moved or gone anywhere while you get lost in the Habits. She's been right here all along, just waiting to embrace you in Her loving, healing arms.

**The Closing Argument.** In the long run, the Victim Habits don't serve you well. The evidence presented is clear, my friend, beyond a reasonable doubt, that life after trauma lies beyond the Victim Habits. Life is found in remembering your true, God-given worth and identity. You are here for a reason; you are no accident. If you have forgotten why you're here (or never discovered it in the first place), well now is the time to dive in and find out.

Spend some time in figuring out your "why." Once you do, the journey to living it out will suddenly appear do-able. In the words of Friedrich Nietzsche:

*"He who has a Why to live for, can bear almost any How."*[15]

The successful shift from victim to victor occurs through faith, courage and a strategic response to victimization. Let's leave the Victim Habits behind where they belong.

# PART THREE

## A STRATEGIC RESPONSE
## TO VICTIMIZATION

-------------------------------------------

# 7

# Priming Yourself to Make the Shift

**The most beautiful people we have known are those who have known defeat, known suffering, known struggle, known loss, and have found their way out of the depths. These persons have an appreciation, a sensitivity, and an understanding of life that fills them with compassion, gentleness, and a deep loving concern. Beautiful people do not just happen.**

*Dr. Elisabeth Kubler-Ross*

Every December and the following January, I enjoy watching the frenetic social psychosis that shows up in the face of a New Year. To make New Year's resolutions, or not. To engage in annual "goal setting," or not. To attend a night of "vision board" making with gal-pals, or not. To join a gym, or not. To sign up for a weight loss program, or not. And on and on it goes.

The trial lawyer in me cracks up at the New Year's "point-counterpoint" posts on social media. I'm an animal of argument. I enjoy taking any side of a debate if there's a formidable opponent willing to play along. (I know what you're thinking...stinking lawyer-types, the odd-balls who think arguing for the sake of arguing is great sport—and you're right.) It's always entertaining to read the posts of "amateurs" and watch them pitch away. Anyway, I digress.

There are posts written with resolve about why it's so great to make resolutions, and what the writer is hell-bent on achieving in the New Year (position of the enamored). Then there are the impassioned declarations about why resolutions should be avoided at all costs; why they are stupid and not worthy of the writer's consideration (position of the disenchanted). I love watching the attempts at persuasion. While the New Year's authors try to convince the world that their position is the right one, the reality is (in my humble opinion) they're really trying to make themselves feel better about their decisions to make (or not make) life changes. For the enamored, I suspect it's a rallying cry, seeking "attagirls" and the gathering of virtual cheerleaders. For the disenchanted, it's a justification for why they've abandoned the New Year's change-game altogether.

So why do the disenchanted become so opposed to New Year's resolutions? More likely than not, they've tried in the past and failed to hit the goal (haven't we all been there?). My take on these disenchanted declarations is that the "failure" in hitting goals, targets, or effecting change was painful. Those who whine and lament about the futility of change simply want to avoid the prospect of "failing again." So what was missing in the campaign to hit a goal and make a change? Usually, quite a few things. The main thing being, *priming*.

**What is Priming?** Priming is the getting ready time, the preparation phase, before taking action. It's really the "action" before "taking action." It's plugging into the power source that propels you forward. It's the motivation, inspiration and initiation to get going every day, taking another step forward toward the goal.

Have you ever had the "privilege" (yes, I'm using that term loosely) of refinishing a piece of furniture? You know, taking that ugly-duckling item you got for a steal at the local garage sale and transforming it? At one particularly ambitious time during my young married life, I decided it was a fantastic idea to purchase a huge farmhouse table built in the Midwest during the 1940s, and turn it into a "showpiece" for my home. Ignoring the facts that I had two small children, had just started my own law practice and was renovating a fixer-upper home, I somehow thought this new project was a good idea. With wild-eyed enthusiasm, I plunked down $50 for the table at a yard sale.

The "new" project table was quite large. It was solid wood, round and had a chunky hand-made pedestal. The table had hundreds of dings and was stained a deep ebony black. Of course, I wanted it to be "shabby chic" and it had to be white. This started the priming. Step one: Stripping the behemoth of all that black stain (we're talking at least 40 hours of stripping, sanding, and stripping some more). Step two: Patching and sanding. Step three: Spraying several coats of primer base paint on the beast. Finally, the table was ready for the beautiful white paint.

Had I not taken the time to go through all that priming, and had I skipped any of the three priming steps, my "diamond in the rough" would have gotten even rougher. The gorgeous swan would never have emerged (which it did, after an enormous amount of blood, sweat, tears, yada yada...). And so it is with making the shift from victim to victor—it all starts with *priming*.

## Priming in Three Simple Steps

As you embark on your journey from victim to victor, there are three simple primers that—when done every day (yes, every day)—will position you to make great strides.

**Priming Step 1: Establish Intentional Daily Rituals, Morning and Night.** You have morning and evening rituals already. How do I know this? Because we are creatures of rituals, either intentional or unintentional. Notice what you do pretty consistently, every morning. It may look like this: Open eyes, grab cell phone, check time. Get out of bed, hit the potty, brush teeth. Head to kitchen, grab coffee, sit on couch and surf online. Hit shower, do hair and makeup, throw on clothes, kiss the dog goodbye, rush to work.

Think about your typical mornings. How often do you truly *veer* from your morning "routine?" If you're like me, there's not a whole lot of veering going on. I used to think I had no "routine" or rituals until I started paying attention to my behaviors. I thought rituals were some big habit-building projects that only the Tony Robbins, Pope and Dalai Lamas of the world built. No, in fact they aren't. That is, if your rituals are unintentional living-by-default routines. The reason you may not realize you already have a morning (and evening) ritual is because our rituals become *automatic*...they're automated. I love this about rituals. (I love anything that can be automated, because it creates less hassle in my world.)

The beauty of creating *intentional rituals* is that when healthy rituals become habits, they free you to focus on higher-level things. Your rituals quietly support your upward trajectory.

**Elements for Great Daily Rituals.** Establishing intentional rituals is a process of trial, adjustment, trial, adjustment. There's no one formula that fits all. For a place to start, below are three actions that, when done each day, tend to foster a joyful state of mind. A joyful state is a forward-looking position, ushering your return from painful life events. Give these a try and modify, add or tweak until you've found a formula that works best for you. These "starter elements" for daily rituals are:

- Breathing;
- Mediation/Prayer; and
- Gratitude.

***Breathing.*** Breathing plays a significant role in shifting your "state." State is all about how you physically and mentally feel, and breathing is a big player in moving out of a fear state to a state of excitement (and who doesn't want to feel excited about life?). We have the absolute ability to take charge of fear and shift that fear into an exhilaration machine.

Legendary psychiatrist Dr. Fritz Perls (founder of Gestalt therapy) gets right to it: "Fear is excitement without the breath..." he declared (and the science backs him up). Dr. Perls studied and made the connection between fear and breathing. He found that the same physical mechanisms in our bodies that produce excitement also produce fear—what an interesting connection! High-performance psychologist and coach Gay Hendricks advocates—in his book *The Big Leap: Conquer Your Hidden Fear and Take Life to the Next Level*—for using Dr. Perls' findings to use fear to our advantage.[16]

The Perls' findings reveal that *fear* can be lessened and transformed when you fully breathe *with it* and *through it*. Did you know that when you're in a fear state, you tend to hold your breath? Notice your body's reaction next time you get freaked out about something. When we experience fear, we immediately respond, in an attempt to stop feeling afraid. Commonly, that response is holding our breath. The problem is, holding your breath has the opposite effect. The less you breathe, you feed the fear and it gets bigger. The more you breathe, fear starts to dissipate and your mental state starts to shift toward excitement. Master this art of breathing through fear, and you'll watch the excitement turn into *exhilaration*.

*Breathing Quick-starter.* As part of my morning ritual (and I am one of those 4:00 a.m. risers), I spend about 10 to 15 minutes doing concentrated breathing exercises, plus prayer and gratitude exercises (discussed below). The breathing part literally takes me about three minutes or less. I call it my "three minutes of power" and the results are phenomenally more enjoyable than wasting time online or listening to the news!

I've found that incorporating breathing exercises into my evening ritual is also very impactful, but the evening exercises are different than the morning. I learned my morning exercises from personal and business mastery coach Tony Robbins, and boy does it work for me. It goes like this (check out the visual in Diagram 1 below to get the gist):

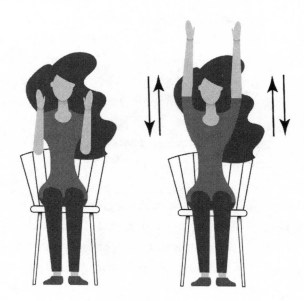

*Diagram 1*

I sit on my outdoor patio couch with my feet flat on the floor (being outside is the best; thank God for Southern California life). I bend my elbows with my palms up, just in front of my shoulders. Then I take a deep breath in through my nose, extending my arms to the sky with my palms while exhaling through my nose. I inhale through the nose as I bring my arms back down to the starting position. This is repeated in rapid sets of 30, until I've done three sets (for a total of 90). In between each set, I rest my forearms on my legs with my palms up, and notice the tingling and energized sensation created by the breathing. This takes a little practice to get the breathing coordinated, so starting out slow is a good idea.

There are plenty of ways to practice morning breathing in a way that gets you primed for the day. The method above may not be for you. The point is, look into breathing and find what *does* work for you. It's truly a game changer.

I've found that ending the day with intentional breathing is really helpful to restful sleep and productive reflection on the day. For me, about two minutes of slow inhaling breaths through the nose, holding for five seconds, then long exhales through the mouth are helpful. During inhale/exhale, I think of something that happened during the day that I feel good about, and say a prayer of thanks.

*Meditation/Prayer.* By now you've probably guessed that I'm a believer in the power of prayer. But even if you don't consider yourself a "religious" or "spiritual" person, I invite you to be open to this idea. My morning ritual includes prayer. You may do something similar, but call it meditation. For me, sitting for a few calm, quiet moments in the morning and listening for the Still Small Voice is transformational. Without fail, the Creator shows up. This is also a time where I read a few scriptures, journal, and ask God for help with the challenges of the moment.

Your time in quiet reflection, meditation, prayer is a great time to focus on all that is good, ask for guidance and overall, just quiet your mind. When we take time for stillness, we make room for mental clarity. Over the years, I've learned that prayer is a two-way street. I don't have to talk God's ears off. Being quiet allows creative solutions to rise up. Being quiet is grounding. It takes a little practice, but over time and with patience, the payoffs are huge.

A common occurrence in meditation is mind-wandering. Even more so now than ever, there's a constant barrage of information and external stimuli (I can't even go to the gas station without video screens on the pumps bombarding me with ads and useless noise). If you find your mind wandering to negative spaces, you may want to try reciting a scripture or mantra each time the wandering starts up. For example, if you quiet yourself down, close your eyes and start thinking of all the stuff the day may bring, that's the time to stop the wander-mind in its tracks. Open your eyes, read your mantra/scripture, close your eyes and repeat it to yourself a few times.

Quiet reflection takes *practice*, so give it some time. You'll get better at it each day. One of the easiest ways to start in prayer and meditation is to simply think of three or four things you are grateful for, and softly say "thank you" out loud. It might look like this:

*"Thank you for this home. I am grateful to have a safe, warm place to lay my head at night."*

*"Thank you for my car. I am grateful for reliable transportation to take to work each day."*

*"Thank you for the sunrise. I am grateful for a new day with fresh possibilities."*

Gratitude is an essential part of daily rituals that *heal*. Gratitude isn't limited to meditation; but when you flex that gratitude muscle during daily prayer/meditation time, it supercharges the experience.

**Gratitude.** Gratitude is an amazing soul-balm. The most charming, successful and charismatic people I've known are those who approached life with an overwhelming attitude of gratitude. These have been some of the happiest and fulfilled people I've ever encountered. And many have experienced severe life challenges, only you'd never know it based on their outlook. Gratitude transformed their outlook, and their zest for life was infectious. What was the secret?

The secret is *choice*. Living through the lens of gratitude is an intentional act. Gratitude-filled living is the result of *saper vedere,* Italian for "knowing how to see." The phrase *saper vedere* was coined by master artist Leonardo da Vinci, as he described his visualization process for the drawing and design of his great works. Much like da Vinci's visualization process, when gratitude is practiced over time, you will learn and *know how to see* the many blessings, kindnesses, gifts and generosities extended to you by others and by God. *Saper vedere* is developed through practice, consistently and every day (just like a great artist does to hone his craft).

Gratitude, when baked into our morning and evening rituals, reduces anxiety. It provides perspective on how much in life you truly have. Gratitude shifts your focus from all that is "wrong" in life, to the higher perspective of all that is truly right and good. So how do you develop your gratitude muscle?

- *Mediation/Prayer "Top Three."* As discussed above, pick the top three things or people you are so thankful for and say out loud, "Thank you for...(Sally), I am so appreciative that...(she cares about me and calls me nearly every day)."

- *Gratitude Tokens.* These are physical things that remind you to stop and notice your blessings. My longtime friend, O.B. Johnson (now a delightful octogenarian) always carries a small, smooth round stone in his pocket. He calls it his gratitude rock. O.B. shows me his gratitude rock every time I see him. He says that every time he puts his hand in his pocket he feels that rock. He turns it over in his palm, feels the cool, soothing smooth stone and says a prayer of thanks for something in his life. As you may imagine, O.B. is a beautiful soul and he is well-loved in the community. He's been a wildly successful commercial real estate broker for decades, served on the boards of many successful nonprofits and start-ups, and is a well-known mover and shaker. Gratitude is O.B.'s secret superpower.

- *Magic Moments.* In a journal, write down at least three positive things that happened in the last 24 hours that you feel good about. It can be a big thing, a not-so-big thing or anything at all…as long as you felt good or happy about it. Be sure to note what the moment was, and *how* that moment, accomplishment or event made you feel. Examples:

*I scheduled that doctor's appointment I'd been putting off for months. This made me feel relieved to get it done. I feel good about prioritizing my health. It felt productive.*

*My spouse and I planned a date night and had an amazing time. I feel great about making time to nurture my marriage. It felt wonderful to reconnect with my spouse.*

*I created an awesome presentation and pitched it to a prospective client, and got the account. I feel very accomplished to have done the work to make the presentation great. I'm proud of myself for stepping out of my comfort zone to pitch this high-level client. I feel great about landing such a big account.*

When you look at the good things happening in your life (and they're there, waiting for you to notice them), it's like waving a magic wand. And when you notice how you *feel* about those good things, that's where the "magic" happens. It changes your state from weighed down to optimistic. From hopeless to hopeful. You begin to realize that good things are happening all around you. As you look at your Magic Moments, say "thank you" to God, the Universe (or whatever you want to call it) for those moments. Magic Moments teach us "how to see" and *saper vedere* happens.

- *Tell Someone How Much You Appreciate Them.* When you say good morning to your co-workers, when you drop your kids off at school, or say goodbye to your spouse as they head out the door, tell them one thing you appreciate about them as part of your gratitude rituals. In the evening, try making a quick phone call to a friend or a parent (or shoot out a brief email or text) and express your gratitude for them. There's something about verbalizing your gratitude for and to others that resets perspective and focus.

**Priming Step 2: Make a Conscious Decision to Take Action.** Moving out of a victim mindset starts with a decision. There is power in deciding what you want your future to look like, clarifying your decision on paper, and declaring it to yourself and to those who support you. Take 30 minutes and answer these key questions, to help you make the very conscious decision to move forward, and get clear on what you really want:

A. *Identity Questions.* Our lives mirror what we believe to be true about ourselves. Regardless of what you've been believing, today you have the ability to redefine what is true about yourself. Deciding to cast off limiting beliefs about yourself and stand in the *truth* of who you were meant/made to be is transformative. It's about making the decision to challenge the identity you've adopted for yourself, and cast off the parts that are not true or helpful. This stage of priming is one of the first steps to remembering (or truly discovering once and for all) who you *truly are*, apart from the life challenges you've experienced. So, first decide and then *challenge* all that you believe about yourself:

1. *How have you been defining yourself?*

   Think about yourself in the third person. Imagine you're an outsider, an observer (the "Observer-You"). Observer-You is looking at you, seeing how you move about your days, and hearing the words you say to yourself.

   a. How would Observer-You describe what she/he is seeing as they observe you?

   b. Based on what the Observer-You is seeing, what would she/he reasonably conclude you believe about yourself?

2. *What identity would make you feel great about yourself?*

   a. What identity would make you feel hopeful about your future?

   b. What untrue, limiting beliefs have you been accepting about yourself?

   c. What beliefs about yourself will set you free to experience an extraordinary life?

3. *Write down those new, liberating beliefs you have decided to start believing about yourself today (in place of the untrue, limiting beliefs).*

B. *"What Do You Want?" Questions.* The beauty of remembering your *true identity* in the midst of life challenges (and after) is you begin to get clear on what you really *want* in life. It's this clarity that leads you to living out your great purpose.

I've always believed that when we're doing things we carry a great passion for, fulfilling the motivations that truly *drive* us, we are doing what we were placed on the planet to do. There's a reason you get particularly jazzed about certain things. When you're living and doing things in your passion zone, you typically do those things *best*. It's what you're meant to do.

So to answer the question, "what do I really want?" the best place is to start with what charges your batteries. So many people don't take time to *design* their own lives! Instead, they react to day-to-day external demands and watch life pass them by. This is the ultimate drifting, and it's no way to live. You were designed for so much more. If you're ready to take your life back, let's drill down on what it is you'd really like your life to look like (right away!):

1. *What do you love?*
   a. For a moment, cast aside all your fears, doubts, shame, anger, negative feelings. Think about something that feels meaningful to you. What is it?
   b. What are you passionate about?
   c. Assume you cannot fail—who do you want to be?
2. *Knowing what you're passionate about, and what makes you feel hopeful about the future, what do you really want?*
   a. What does a remarkable life look like for you in the next 12 months (what will you get, experience, get free from, do)?
3. *What will the pay-offs be when those things become true for you?*

4. *What would have to be true for those things to happen?*
   a. What do you need to believe about yourself for those things to happen?
5. *What is preventing you from making that remarkable life happen?*
6. *What needs to change right now to make it happen?*
   a. What actions can you take right now to change it?

All the questions above are organized for you in the *Priming Checklist and Prep Sheet* bonus that appears in Appendix A at the end of this book. I've also created a digital version for you on VictimIsNotYourName.com, where you can use this fillable form as often as you like, as you grow through this process. As you complete the Identity and Wants Questions, you'll end up with a solid, conscious decision about what you want in your life for the next six to 12 months. And as you look at the end results, the *action plan* will appear. After all, you'll identify the immediate shifts you need to make to remove the barriers to the life you want. In identifying what needs to change, suddenly you've got an action plan!

**Priming Step 3: Get in the Right Lane.** This is about mastering your thoughts and your focus. You want to prime yourself each morning to get in the right lane (and stay there). Staying in the right "lane" gives you the mental support to keep moving forward. This is like doing the last round of sanding on that table before you lay down a coat of primer paint. Do this each day, and you'll significantly *reduce* anxiety, *reduce* worrying and avoid getting yourself into a low-energy state of mind (think, frustration, overwhelm, defeat).

What are we talking about here? Getting into the right lane is all about consciously staying in your zones of *empowerment*. In Stephen Covey's classic *The 7 Habits of Highly Effective People,* he introduced the "Circles of Influence and Control."[17] The idea is simple: Every concern or situation we're thinking about falls into one of four zones. Two zones are *empowering*; the other two, *disempowering*.

Let's go, zone-by-zone, lane-by-lane. I want you to think about something that's been on your mind. Something you've been thinking about, *a lot*. Got it? Okay then, we'll call it "Your Thing." Look at Diagram 2 below:

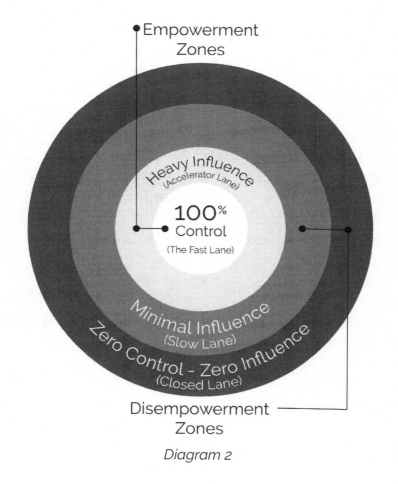

*Diagram 2*

The Fast Lane: *"Stuff I Have 100% Control Over."* This is in the bullseye, and it's an *empowerment zone*. I call this The Fast Lane, because when you spend most of your time here, it fast-tracks you to living an extraordinary life.

The stuff you have absolute control over is a very small set of things. Think for a moment about what you have absolute control over, and make a list. (No really, do it now.) How long is your list? I'll bet it didn't get past four or five things.

Now, about Your Thing. Ask yourself, "Is this something I have any control over?" If the answer is "no" then you're not in this zone. That doesn't necessarily mean you're in a disempowerment zone. First we have to ask the next question (but *do notice* that Your Thing isn't in the 100% control zone).

The Accelerator Lane: "*Stuff I Have Little or No Control Over, but I Have a Great Deal of Influence Over.*" This is the next smallest ring, and it's also an *empowerment zone*. This is where the ultimate outcome is beyond your absolute control, but you can heavily influence that outcome. An example of this is what I do as a trial lawyer (and the main reason people pay me "the big bucks").

If you were to go into court asking the judge to make an order in your favor, as a layperson you would realize very quickly that you have no control over the proceedings or the outcome. Neither do I, as an attorney. But what I *do have* that the non-lawyer doesn't is a great deal of *influence* over the *outcome* of those proceedings. My significant influence is a result of my training, skills and experience—something the non-lawyer simply doesn't have. It's what I do. But ultimately, I do not have absolute control over the proceedings because it is a judge (or a jury) who controls the final result (they decide). We all know that no matter what the facts are in a case, how well-prepared or persuasive the attorneys are, and how credible the witnesses are (or aren't), judges and juries routinely make decisions that surprise us.

Regardless of your opinion, the "Trial of the Century" (O.J. Simpson), the Michael Jackson child molestation case, and the Casey

Anthony acquittal of her daughter Caylee Anthony's death all had the same thing in common: Despite the very best efforts of prosecutors, the not-guilty verdicts handed down were shocking to millions of viewers following those trials. Why? Because at the end of the day, the judges and juries in those cases were *influenced* one way or the other, but at no time were they *controlled* by either side in the case.

The point is, when the outcome of Your Thing is something you can't absolutely control, but your actions can directly *influence* the outcome, you're definitely still in an empowerment zone. I call this The Accelerator Lane, because when you spend time exerting significant influence over the result you're seeking, you're moving toward your intended results (and you increase the likelihood that you'll get them). The great news is, instead of worrying about Your Thing, you can *do something about* Your Thing and that's worth the effort.

The Slow Lane: "*Stuff I Have No Control Over and Only Minimal Influence Over.*" This is the second largest ring. It's a large ring because a lot of what people worry about and fuss over are things in this ring and in the largest ring ( "Zero Control, Zero Influence").

Is Your Thing an issue that's both out of your control *and* something you have little to no influence over? If so, why are you bothering? Ask yourself, "Is it time to let go of this?" This analysis is something that truly deserves your attention (unless it's "fun" for you).

I call this The Slow Lane because spending my time and energy here slows me down from getting to where I'm going—the next level of creating an extraordinary life. It's like getting behind a big old diesel truck going up a steep incline. You'll take your foot off the accelerator and your state will shift (guaranteed). In most instances, the best course of action is to change lanes. Start up again in the lanes where you can actually affect the outcome and stop wasting time in The Slow Lane. Spending a great deal of time here will suck the life out of you, because it's disempowering…to the max.

The Closed Lane: "*Stuff I Have No Control Over and No Influence Over.*" This one is the ultimate dead zone. It's like boarding a jumbo jet from Los Angeles to Paris and worrying the whole 11 hours about the plane falling out of the sky. Unless you're the pilot, there's not a hill of beans you can do about it. Is Your Thing in The Closed Lane? You know, the lane where there's no driving at all because it's shut down for repairs?

Here's the bottom line: If Your Thing is in either of these outer rings, you're up to your neck in *disempowerment* and it's not where you want to be. We are disempowered when there's nothing we can do about the situation, and yet we focus on it.

As you prime each day, be very aware of your thoughts, concerns and energy. Notice where they're focused and make a course-correction if you find yourself in The Slow Lane or The Closed Lane. If there's a life circumstance that you can neither control nor significantly influence the outcome of, the best you can do is make contingency plans for the most probable positive and negative outcomes of things in this zone. Do what you *can* control and surrender the rest.

With practice and consistent priming, you'll build a strong infrastructure to support your next move...disrupting the Victim Habit. Commit to patience. Decide that life is happening *for* you, not *to* you. You're off to a solid start. Bright future, here YOU come!

# 8

# Disrupting the Victim Habit

**Disruptive movement must come from within.**

*Leo Tolstoy*

Disruption has been a hot topic in business over the last decade. Why? Because disruption has led to significant transformation and innovation. Those who've decided to get comfortable with the uncomfortable have become industry leaders. They've snuffed out the competition, almost like a "sneak attack"—by challenging the status quo, introducing new ways of doing things—innovative ideas that met customers' needs and wants, before consumers even demanded it.

Successful industry disruptors all brought an element of surprise to the game. Their competition never saw it coming. That's because so many in business are lulled into complacency by the seeming security and stability that comes from doing the same thing and staying in the same place...leaving cutting edge "innovation" and evolving customer needs behind. One of the most well-known disruptors in the last 20 years is Netflix. In the late 90s, this innovator turned the home video rental industry on its head by delivering DVDs right to customers' mailboxes. Netflix eliminated the customer's need to go to a video store to rent movies. This disruption of how we rented movies put the Blockbuster Video chain out of business in no time.

Disruption really isn't about creativity or pure innovation—those ideas stand on their own. In the context of Victim Habits, disruption is about flipping the status quo on its head; interrupting those behavioral patterns that no longer serve you. How do you begin the effective disruption of Victim Habits? By gaining a clear vision of how your life will go, and the opportunities waiting for you when the Habits no longer play a leading role in your life.

Without disruption, the Victim Habits keep us in a perpetual state of imprisonment, much like the 1993 film "Groundhog Day," where actor Bill Murray would wake up each morning, only to repeat the same thing day in and day out. Without disruption, Victim Habits keep you distracted from living out your true calling. Simply put, lack of disruption equals *distraction*.

A few years ago, a man in his late 50s sought my help in his very sad divorce case. He had been married for 35 years and had been in an emotionally abusive marriage. A few years before, Dennis (of course, not his real name) had been injured at work and went out on permanent disability.

During our first meeting in my office, Dennis' physical and emotional pain were palpable. He could barely sit for more than 10 minutes. His medications made it hard for him to focus and at times, great effort was required to pull up the words.

The final straw that broke the marriage, Dennis described, was another heated argument with his overbearing wife Joan. The argument escalated to the point that Joan lost it, and threw a heavy object at his head (and thankfully missed). The police were called and the ugly incident resulted in a restraining order against Joan, where she was ordered to immediately move out of the family home. Joan was the bread winner, no surprise in light of Dennis' permanent disability.

Dennis, as sad as his story was, turned out to be a big red flag as law clients go. He came to me as a referral from a prominent pastor in town, who often refers people to me and of course, I value the trust the pastor places in the work we do. Like my attorney-daughter Rachael's decision to try to help Lola (described in Chapter Four, in case you're jumping around in this book...), I decided to help Dennis because I felt sorry for him. But Dennis was trouble from the beginning. He'd gone through three other lawyers in the 11 months before he came to see me, and he bent my law team's ear on the phone for an unreasonable amount of time before he even made the first appointment.

Why was Dennis full of red flags for the lawyers? Well as the facts unfurled, they revealed a mess of legal relationships all destroyed by Dennis' Victim Habits. When challenging issues in his case came up, Dennis would go MIA. He just didn't want to deal with it, so he buried his head and got real creative in the narratives he crafted to justify his behavior. Dennis began to treat his attorneys' staff members with utter rudeness and disdain. He acted like everyone was out to get him.

To make matters worse, when Dennis didn't want to participate in certain court hearings—because he was afraid or stressed about the possible outcome—he would send long, rambling emails in the middle of the night, coming up with every creative excuse for why he could not participate. The interesting part was that Dennis would employ extreme *victim lingo* and would spend *hours and hours* crafting his long emails. Dennis went to great lengths to explain how stressed, ill and unable he was—all to justify his refusal to communicate and refusal to participate in the parts of his own case that he didn't care to do. This was very destructive behavior. Dennis would spend nearly *twice the time and effort* to write his long victim manifesto emails as it would to just have participated in the meeting, the hearing, the conversation or whatever it was he was resisting doing.

For example, his wife's attorney had scheduled Dennis' deposition and the date was coming up. A deposition is where a meeting of the attorneys and the parties happens, usually in the conference room of one of the attorneys' offices, and testimony is taken and recorded by a court reporter. We use depositions to quickly get information from the other party, under oath, about what their claims are, and to unearth the evidence that supports their claims. This gets us ready for trial.

So with Dennis' deposition rapidly approaching, I needed to meet with him to prepare for the short, three hour deposition. But Dennis was hell-bent on *not* attending. After several weeks of leaving voicemail messages, sending emails, texts and snail-mail, I *finally* heard from Dennis. Below is only an *excerpt* from the *seven page* email I received. Notice the repeated victim labels Dennis uses, and notice how "in the past" Dennis operates. In a nutshell, he's stuck on rewind.

Keep in mind, at the time he wrote this Dennis hadn't actually seen or interacted with his wife Joan for over a year, since Joan got hit with a restraining order. In fact, just two months before this email, Dennis had moved out of the marital home he had shared with Joan because the court ordered the house be sold. Dennis moved into a guest casita at the estate of some friends from his church. He was in a comfortable, rent-free (and temporary) living situation. Nearly $500,000 from the sale of Joan and Dennis' home was sitting in a blocked account, to be divided between them when the divorce case was over:

*Kelly,*

*I've developed a new medical condition in addition to my unending, devastating medical conditions and disabilities which are getting worse by the minute! On top of all that, you need to remember that I'm a mess. I'm still dealing with the aftermath of severe emotional trauma and the life-long side effects of domestic violence and having lived with an abusive spouse.*

*Therefore, it's not in my best interest to be subjected to unnecessary stressors like prolonged, tortuous questioning from Joan's attorney. Just like Joan, her attorney is unethical. He's been mean, condescending and very aggressive in the way he speaks to me. If I am forced to deal with him, this will be very harmful—this must be avoided at all costs!*

*This deposition thing is more abuse. When will it stop? It's more harassment by Joan. You need to understand that a deposition is unnecessary and harmful to my physical health, my medical conditions, and my overall emotional well-being. You must protect me!*

*You need to stop everything and ask the court to intervene. Make the judge STOP JOAN. Again, I'm telling you that a deposition will seriously hurt me—both emotionally and physically. Even spiritually—I just know it! My friends can testify to how damaged I am. They all advise me to refuse to allow all this stress in my life—why aren't you protecting me?*

*Joan financially abused me by making me have to protect myself through a restraining order. This was more abuse, having to get a restraining order even though I'm disabled. My finances are a wreck because I had to pay legal fees with my first attorney to get the restraining order. As a result of Joan's financial abuse and all this continuing emotional trauma, I'm certain that in the end, I'll have no money for my medical expenses and little to no money to take care of my bare necessities. I'll be poverty stricken for the rest of my life. I've probably only got a few short years left, with all the trauma I've been through.*

*You need to make the judge understand how important it is to see my needs. He needs to remember that I'm a victim of domestic violence and severe medical conditions. Make him see how disabled I am and how bad my emotional health is because of that domestic abuse from Joan. You need to point out that I've also been abused by Joan's family members too, because they support her and not me...the judge should be asked to limit Joan's actions. If he doesn't, I will be seriously and negatively affected in this discovery method of deposition.*

*Besides, since I was forced to move out of my house, I don't really know where all the documents are that they have demanded me to bring to a deposition. They're in boxes somewhere—so I won't be able to bring them to a deposition anyway. Physically I'm not in any shape to look for anything—it was tiring enough for me to pack when I moved. So, tell the judge and Joan's lawyer that I can't find anything due to pain and my physical limitations.*

*The judge needs to protect me from Joan's humiliating conduct and her continuing abuse. All this abuse is going to happen if Joan's attorney gets ahold of any of my medical records or sees my personal finances. How I spent our life savings over the last year is none of Joan's business! After all, she was the one who threw a paperweight at my head, so she's the perpetrator and perpetrators shouldn't have the right to complain about how I spent the money. If her attorney gets that information, I just know that later on he and Joan will re-victimize me by using that information in some illegal and abusive way.*

*Kelly, you need to get on this right away. You need to be aggressive to stop the further downward spiral of my health. You have to understand that now, I'm for sure not well at all. My life has been destroyed and I'll never have a decent quality of life. I'm not going to a deposition.*

*Dennis*

Now before you think, "Good grief Kelly! This guy really needs help..." know that I agree with you. He needs a great deal of help first and foremost—with his *mindset.* The best thing he could have done for himself would be to *disrupt* his Victim Habits and deal with his discomfort.

You know what's interesting about the timing of that email from Dennis? The *truth.* The facts are that when Dennis wrote his victim manifesto, the one-year restraining order against his wife had long expired. Restraining orders are regularly renewed when the restrained person continues to pose a threat. There was no threat; in fact, Joan couldn't stay far enough away from Dennis—she was "over it" and had moved on. It's by no means right that Joan threw a paperweight at Dennis. But the reality is, this was the only incident of physical aggression during their 35-year marriage. The other incongruent truths were that Dennis could drive, he was regularly taking himself to church functions and mid-week Bible studies. He was regularly going grocery shopping on his own and he spent a great deal of time online, using Attorney Google to study the law and serve as an arm-chair lawyer.

Don't get me wrong. I really cared about Dennis. A lot of the time he was, quite frankly...hard to like and hard to love. He was prickly. Most of the time Dennis wasn't intellectually honest when he didn't care for the facts or the law. Occasionally I wondered out loud if Dennis saw the phrase "stupid" stamped across my forehead, based on the disingenuous things he tried to pull over on my law office. But at the end of the day, Dennis had a bright future ahead of him, *if* he would only choose to *disrupt* his victim-project and do something different. Dennis was a prolific writer. Dennis had a good analytical mind and was quick to grasp complex ideas, especially legal theories as I explained them to him. Dennis was college-educated, *smart and very capable* of doing a lot of things, despite his injury and despite having an unpleasant jerk of an ex-wife.

Where is Dennis now? Well, his Victim Habits got in the way of our relationship, to the point that I was unable to do my job for him. Dennis is still dragging out his divorce case, years after it started. He chose to represent himself, and he's not doing a very impressive job of it.

The shift for Dennis will come when he decides to *disrupt* his Victim Habits. This means facing his fears associated with stepping into his full potential. It means changing his physiology to move from fear to *excitement* about stepping up. It means recognizing his victim-oriented thinking patterns, and replacing them with a *growth mindset*. This is about thinking of yourself more as a hammer, rather than the nail.

# 9

# Six Paths to
# Utter Disruption

**If you can't fly then run, if you can't run then walk,
if you can't walk then crawl, but whatever you do
you have to keep moving forward.**

*Dr. Martin Luther King, Jr.*

There are a lot of ways to disrupt the Victim Habit. Some
ways are simple, others more creative. There is no one "right
way" to disrupt a pattern of behavior, other than trying as
many things as it takes to find what works. The six disruption tactics below are some of the most effective approaches I've seen (and
implemented). Try one, a few, or all of them. You've got nothing to
lose. Let's start with the easiest, and build to the beefiest of strategies:

## Disruptor #1: Transform Your Environment

Disrupting Victim Habits starts with mental clarity. Clarity is all
about eliminating the "noise" and focusing on what really *matters*.

One big "noise" factor is an unsupportive *physical* environment, at home and at work. Look around you (yes, right now). What does your personal home space look like? Is it comforting? Relaxing? Orderly? How about your work environment? Is your work space clean and organized, or do piles of chaos whap you across the face each morning? Our environments are worth paying attention to because they play a big role in supporting a calm, centered, victor state of mind. Not only does our physical environment directly affect our moods and feelings, how we *keep* our environments says a lot about us.

**The Role of Your Physical Environment.** When our surroundings are messy, full of clutter, dirt or dust, we naturally feel *chaotic*. Without a doubt, it's stressful. Have you ever toured new model homes? It's a pretty enjoyable experience, and it feels good to walk into a clean new home that's "all together." What you notice is the lack of clutter and distraction. It's peaceful...it's devoid of *noise.*

When I was in college, I remember chatting with my roommate Christian about looking for a job for the upcoming summer. Christian was from Texas, where her father ran the family business, and where Christian always had a summer job waiting. It was there that Christian's father taught her some crazy-great life lessons in the process.

I was around 19 or 20 when Christian told me about her dad's approach to hiring. When a job applicant was scheduled for an interview, Christian's dad would sit her down, tell her the name of the applicant and what time he or she was to arrive. Christian was assigned the task of watching the parking lot for the applicant's arrival. When the candidate was settled into the conference room for the interview, Christian was then to go into the parking lot and peek through the windows of the candidate's car. She would then report back to her father about what she observed. Was the car tidy and clean? Were there signs of a food-fest inside? Were there papers and trash strewn about? How clean was the car on the outside?

Christian's father explained the meaning of the task to her. He said, "you can tell a lot about a person by looking in their car. If someone comes to a job interview looking spiffy in their Sunday best, hair combed and shoes shined, a dirty, sloppy car is a big sign of what's really going on in their mind; in their approach to life." I was really surprised to hear that an employer would read that much into the car thing, but as I grew older and began to grow my own business I learned how insightful Christian's father was in his approach to hiring. After implementing the "look in the car" approach, I've discovered that there is much to the idea that a cluttered space is the sign of a cluttered mind. Simply put, clutter compromises clarity.

You don't need a lot of money to create a supportive environment at both work and home. But is it clean and organized? Are the closets jammed with stuff you never use, or are the essentials neat and easy to find? To me, a clean and organized environment is essential. I even carry this approach to my environment when I'm travelling.

Several years ago, my sister Mindy and I travelled to Charleston, South Carolina, for a long "sisters' weekend"—just the two of us. We booked ourselves into a beautiful boutique hotel in the heart of old Charleston. The hotel was a stunner.

As we entered our room, we noticed how big and beautiful it was, with a high attention to detail throughout. It was immediately calming and relaxing. I scouted out the closet and dresser drawers and divvied the space up between my sister and me. Then I got right to work unpacking the suitcase, neatly hanging up my clothes and putting my underthings and socks neatly in the drawers.

Mindy, on the other hand, threw her bulging suitcase on an armchair and flopped onto the bed. A few minutes later we decided to head out to find a great place for dinner. As we changed our clothes, Mindy flung open her suitcase and began digging through it to find an outfit. As she dug, Mindy plopped piles of clothes on the floor next to her bag. And that's the method sis used the entire four days

100 | Victim Is Not Your Name

we were in Charleston. Not a single article of clothing landed in the closet or in the dresser!

And I remember it to this day, because every time we came into the hotel room, that messy little corner of the room—the chaos of the "open air closet"—hit me like a ton of bricks. It stressed me out. It was like a pimple on the face of perfect little porcelain doll!

Before you think I'm really dogging on my little sister here, let me explain. At this stage of her life, Mindy was a thirty-something mom of four children in a very blended family: A 12-year-old step-son; a 14-year-old adopted daughter who had been abused and abandoned throughout her first nine years on the planet; a four-year-old daughter and a two-year-old son. Mindy would go on to have a fifth child, a beautiful daughter born with special needs.

On top of the house full of young children, Mindy was married to a DIY, home improvement fanatic. The husband loved ripping up Mindy's house to add new windows, move walls, and create new spaces. However, he had a very bad habit of never finishing what he started. The inside of Mindy's house was one big construction zone, constantly in a state of chaos. Explains a lot, right?

Over the years, my sister recognized the contribution of a chaotic environment to her internal overwhelm. Mindy's made huge changes in her life, including cleaning out the clutter (environmental and marital). Her environment now is neat and clean. And she's gone on to get a post-graduate degree, and pursued an amazing career in cancer imaging for one of the country's leading medical research hospitals. What a difference!

**Your Turn.** So how about you? Is your home space a comforting sanctuary after a busy day? Does your personal workspace "welcome" you each morning? Whether you're already a neatnik or a prime candidate for the next season of *Hoarders,*[18] there's always room for improvement. Just *start*.

If you've allowed your space to become uninspiring, I recommend using the KonMari Method™ developed by organizing expert Marie Kondo. Marie is an amazing tidying expert, who espouses: "Start by discarding. Then organize your space, thoroughly, completely, in one go."[19]

After working with hundreds of clients, helping them go from messy to tidy, Marie says, "...there is one thing I can say with confidence: A dramatic reorganization of the home causes correspondingly dramatic changes in lifestyle and perspective. It is life transforming... everyone who completes my private course [on tidying] has successfully kept their house in order—with unexpected results. Putting their house in order positively affects all other aspects of their lives, including work and family." Marie goes on to quote a few testimonials from her clients, like:

> *"...[Putting my house in order] taught me to see what I really need, and what I don't. So I got a divorce. Now I feel much happier."*

> *"I'm delighted to report that since cleaning up my apartment, I've been able to really increase my sales."*

> *"I'm amazed to find that just throwing things away has changed me so much."[20]*

Support your new way of thinking by living in beautiful, uncluttered spaces. Let the disruption begin!

## Disruptor #2: Get Moving

Sometimes, our Victim Habits foster physical lethargy. You know, those days off work when you stay in the pajamas all morning...

morning turns into afternoon, and before you know it, it's time for bed and you're a big, smelly mess. Lethargy sucks. It masquerades as a comforting idea that you *deserve* some down time, lounge time, couch time. Ever notice that at the end of a "jammie day," you don't feel particularly refreshed or fulfilled? That's because lethargy, slow states (really *all states of mind*) are self-perpetuating. They want to grow legs and take over, and they will unless they are *mastered.*

Movement is a really effective antidote to Victim Habits, because physical movement keeps the mind moving *forward.* There's a great deal of research in human physiology that makes the case for movement. Movement is like hitting the reset button on your psychology. Just Google "psychological benefits of exercise" and you'll be gobsmacked by the amount of evidence out there, telling you to *move!*

Medical researchers from Duke University looked at the long-term effects of exercise on patients suffering from major depression. The extensive study started with already-established findings that 30 minutes of brisk exercise just three times per week was *just as effective* as drug "therapy" was in relieving symptoms of major depression, in the short term. But what about the long term? This is where it got really interesting: The Duke researchers discovered that continued exercise has *long-lasting* effects on depression, and drastically reduced the chances of depression returning (and no, you don't have to become a triathlete or anything extreme to get these results). In fact, after the study group exercised moderately but consistently over six months, *only eight percent experienced a return of their depressive symptoms.*

Even more surprising in the Duke study, the test groups that used a combination of exercise and anti-depression medications saw lesser results than did the group that dumped the meds and focused on movement. Why? Duke psychologist/researcher James Blumenthal opined that the exercise-only group got better results because they were taking an active role (taking ownership) in getting themselves better:

*Simply taking a pill is very passive...Patients who exercised may have felt a greater sense of mastery over their condition and gained a greater sense of accomplishment. They may have felt more self-confident and competent because they were able to do it themselves, and attributed their improvement to their ability to exercise.*

Dr. Blumenthal went on to note the snowball effect. That is, once the depressed patients started feeling better, they gained momentum and started to exercise *more*, which of course, made them feel even better.[21] This is not to say you should stop taking medications, but with movement comes mental healing—a healing that is worth exploring.

My challenge to you is this: For the next 10 days, when you pop your eyes open in the morning, try saying, out loud, "I want to *thrive today!*" Write it down, put it on your nightstand, and read it out loud to yourself each morning.

Remember the concept discussed early on in this book...your brain and your body will *follow* what you tell it. Focusing on *thriving* instead of "just surviving" will help you jump into disruption mode. Then put on your shoes and walk, or take a break at work and get out into the sunshine and walk, run, bike or whatever floats your boat. For me, it's salt-water therapy. My happy, re-set the mind place is the big blue ocean. When I turn off the depressive talk and put myself in the water—just me, my surfboard and God—the healing begins.

## Disruptor #3: Re-Wire Your Brain

In the last few years, information about the practical application of brain science has become more available to "regular" people (instead of a subject reserved for those brainy medical experts). I've become increasingly curious about brain science—sometimes called neuroscience or neuroplasticity. There's an amazing amount of research in this area and its application to our thinking patterns. Think of the possibilities here: Regardless of what's happened to you in life, you've got an amazing control center in you—your brain—which is open to re-wiring. With re-wiring, imagine the possibilities you hold within your head, for transforming yourself *in spite of* past traumas. What a gift.

Can we really re-wire our brains, and create new patterns of thinking that move us out of despair, low productivity and unhappiness? The answer is a resounding, "100% YES!" and the science backs it up. It's thrilling to know that yes—*absolutely yes*—you've got it in you. You've got significant inner strengths, and they're just like any other muscle. People with seemingly unshakeable inner strength are people who have grown that muscle. They've developed a habit, a pattern of thinking that supports the growth of their inner strengths. In short, they've re-wired their brains to kick the Victim Habit to the curb.

Noted clinical psychologist and neuroscientist, Dr. Rick Hanson, has researched and worked extensively in the area of brain re-wiring. In his book, *"Resilient,"* Dr. Hanson demonstrates how to practically deal with everyday stressors, disappointments and traumas. His research reveals practical methods of how to stop treating past life traumas like they're your destiny:

*True resilience fosters well-being, an underlying sense of happiness, love and peace. Remarkably, as you internalize experiences of well-being, that builds inner strengths which in turn make you more resilient. Well-being and resilience promote each other in an upward spiral.*

***The key is knowing how to turn passing experiences into lasting inner resources built into your brain.*** *This is positive neuroplasticity..."*[22]

As we discussed earlier, habits aren't really things to *break*, as much as they are things to *replace*. And so it goes with Victim Habits—it's about replacing them. What Dr. Hanson suggests is that by tapping into positive past experiences (i.e. positive neuroplasticity), you can replace the Victim Habits with those inner resources which result in true resilience.

**The Brain Versus The Mind.** As you learn from various life experiences, your brain is continually changing, remodeling itself. Our brain is our hardware, the motherboard of our system, if you will. Dr. Hanson describes it like a refrigerator. Your brain is always on, always humming with billions of neurons firing every single minute, in order to keep your body alive and ready to handle your urgent needs.[23]

It has been said that your brain *represents* your mind. So what is the mind? It's not physical but it's still real. Understanding this stuff requires some mental gymnastics, but stay with me here—I promise it's worth the cartwheels!

Your brain works hand-in-hand with your nervous system. Your nervous system presents information to the brain. Then the brain processes it, and the mind comes into play.

Imagine you're walking down the street, and you approach an intersection with a traffic light. That traffic light is a physical *thing*—it exists, along with the energy that's behind the light. On the other hand, when you look at a traffic light and notice its color—red, green, yellow—you attach a *meaning* to the colored light. The *meaning* of a red light is usually, *"I better stop."* The *meaning* of a green light is typically, *"It's my turn to go...."*

The meaning of the light is intangible, but it's still information flowing through your nervous system to your brain. So as you take in the information (there's a light, it's red and I better stop because there's danger coming the other direction), you form *experiences*.

Those *experiences* are comprised of *information*—the flow of thought, where you rest your attention. This is your mind.

Did you know that you can use your mind (those experiences) to engage underlying neuro processes and actually *change your brain*? How is this possible? There's a lot of brain activity going on behind the mind; that flow of thought, the processing of feelings and where you focus your attention.[24]

Science shows that the *repeated patterns* of neural activity leave lasting traces behind, much like water coming down a hillside. Study a dry waterfall. What do you see? The ingrained, shallow "trenches" in the rock, left behind by water flowing consistently, over time.

The bottom line is, *you* have the power inside yourself (all the time) to change your mind for the better, through the re-wiring of the brain. Sound odd? Impossible? Think of it this way. Would you agree that you can change the muscles in your arms and legs through weight training and exercise? Of course, that's a "no-brainer" (punny, I know). So why does changing the brain seem so odd? Here are a few keys to the re-wiring process:

## Key: The Negativity Bias— Recognize, Master and Leverage It.

Negativity bias is a real thing. It's your brain's default setting, which focuses on bad experiences. Negative information and experiences imprint more quickly and stick with us much longer than positive information. Why? Because we are *wired* to protect ourselves from harm. Human beings are wired to pay close attention to danger, because the brain reads danger as a matter of life or death, which was especially true in the earlier, less evolved years of our existence. Imagine the very prevalent dangers of life on earth before firearms, civilized nations, cars, houses, and the comforts of life as we know it. Imagine living in the wild, and all that threatens to prey on you if you're not watching. That's what our brains are naturally wired to do: To protect us. Only, we rarely are in that sort of high-level danger these days.

Negative *emotions* stimulate the "alarm bell" of the brain—often called the "reptilian brain"—which is in your brain stem. Think of your reptilian brain as your brain's watch-dog. This part of the brain is in sentry mode, constantly scanning for harmful information. Your reptilian brain uses approximately seventy-five percent of its neurons looking for, and storing, bad news. "Once it sounds the alarm, negative events and experiences get quickly stored in memory, in contrast to positive events and experiences, which usually need to be held in awareness for a dozen or more seconds to transfer from short-term memory buffers to long-term storage..." says Dr. Hanson.[25] Wow! We actually have to work *harder* (holding the positive "in awareness") to get positive events and experiences to stick with us. This explains that saying, oft cast about in psychological circles, that it takes 10 "atta girl" comments to negate one "you suck" put-down. As Dr. Hanson says, ". . . In effect, our brains are like Velcro for bad experiences but Teflon for good ones."[26]

Negativity bias may be our brain's natural default, but that doesn't mean it can't be overcome. It's about creating a new habit and teaching your brain to respond differently. Research shows that overriding negativity bias starts with self-talk. How do you talk to yourself about your day to day experiences? As you move through your daily life, make a choice to notice and focus on the truly important things— the positive experiences. Remember, you're taking time to hold the positive information "in awareness" (sounds a little new age-y to me, but really we're just talking about getting intentional about what you focus upon).

There's a very useful purpose for the negativity bias; it isn't something to be eradicated. Thank goodness for it! It's that protective filter that allows us to be vigilant, aware of dangers in our environment.

But like any strength, the negativity bias is something to be mastered lest it run amok. In re-wiring our brains, we should be mindful (and challenge our thoughts and emotional responses) of the bias.

Remember my octogenarian friend O.B. and his gratitude rock? Try that small but effective tool. Put a small, smooth rock of your own in your pocket. Get in the habit of taking the rock out every hour or two. Feel the cool, smoothness of its surface. As you turn it over in the palm of your hand, ask yourself "what was great about the last two hours? What am I so very grateful for today?" Train your brain to reflect, with gratitude, on the positive aspects of the day, no matter how small.

The smooth-stone approach is also useful to *disrupt* the brain's default focus on negative emotions and memories. Each time you begin to go down the negative emotion path, pull out that stone. Turn it over and feel its soothing, cool smooth surface…and go down the gratefulness list. Sometimes it's even productive to take a walk or do something that makes it hard to ruminate on a negative conversation or situation. You're becoming *disruptive* to the negativity bias. Win-win!

## Key: Ask Life for Your New Assignment— Then Go Do It.

This one's about choices. A profound and most impactful treatise is Holocaust survivor Viktor Frankl's writing, *Man's Search for Meaning*. Frankl was a psychiatrist who survived Auschwitz and other concentration camps in Nazi Germany. His divine insight wrung from living as a prisoner and observing his fellow prisoners is an amazing gift to anyone who's experienced suffering.

The Nazis infamously stripped their prisoners of every worldly possession; their own clothes, their names, their identities. They reduced their prisoners to barely breathing skeletons, with numbers tattooed on them for identification—and that was all. Dr. Frankl noted that while seemingly everything can be taken from a man, his life in the concentration camp proved that there was *one thing* that could never be taken away, "...the last of the human freedoms—to choose one's attitude in any given set of circumstances, to choose one's own way." Dr. Frankl concluded that every day, every hour, we are given the opportunity to decide whether or not we will become the "plaything of circumstance ..."[27]

So what do you decide to do, instead of allowing yourself to become your circumstances' plaything? Watch this: Instead of looking at Life (put another way...at your Creator) and asking, "What've you got *for me*?"...ask a different question. First, understand that when you look at Life with a view toward what it has to *offer* you, you're missing the future, the hope. The secret of survival that Dr. Frankl observed in the few who survived with remarkable mental strength was their ability to pivot that question. Those remarkable few grabbed onto the future by looking at their circumstances and asking, "What's my *assignment* in all of this?" The pivot was from "what do I get out of this?...to "what's my assignment, the learning, the growth opportunity for me in all of this?" The survivors who were able to see purpose and meaning in life, despite the unimaginable daily horrors of the concentration camps, were those who recognized the abundance of opportunities to add a deeper meaning to their lives *through* their circumstances and suffering.[28]

Frankl discovered that those prisoners who could not see beyond their immediate circumstances—who could not see the opportunity to build their inner strength through their circumstances—were not able to see, nor aim to fulfill, their purpose in life. What became of them? These beings began to suffer an inner, mental decay, followed by rapid physical decay. They became preoccupied with retrospective thoughts; living in the past. Preoccupation with the past was a coping mechanism to avoid the pain of the present, but it was a mental death sentence.

Where are you spending your mental life, your inner thoughts? Are you finding yourself preoccupied with the past—in happier, different times—thus avoiding the growth opportunities in present suffering? The danger is described poignantly by Dr. Frankl: "Instead of taking the camp's difficulties as a test of their inner strength, they did not take their life seriously and despised it as something of no consequence. They preferred to close their eyes and live in the past. Life for such people became meaningless."[29]

Instead of responding to your present circumstances with "life is meaningless. I having nothing to live for. Life has let me down..." the pivot is in order: "Life! What do you expect from me?" Or said another way, "What is the right and noble way to respond to the challenges in my life today? What assignments are you giving me right now (Life, God, Universe) to grow my inner strength and do what's right and honorable?"

What assignment is life giving you today? Will you accept it and get on with it? The task is at hand, and with it comes remarkable opportunities—what a great hope that is—for a *future*.

## *Key: Practice Mindfulness.*

Go back to the priming section in Chapter Seven. Remember the mainstays of a rocking morning routine? Breathing, meditation, gratitude. All three of these practices put you into a state of *mindfulness*. Mindfulness is the gateway to re-wiring your brain to rest on those positive, resourceful experiences that disrupt the negativity bias and the overall Victim Habits. Think about what you're focusing your attention on when you engage in the breathing exercises, in meditation and gratitude; those things that create positive mental resources in your brain.

# Disruptor #4: Rebuild Your Inner Circle

Who's in your inner circle? These are the people you allow to be closest to you. The people you share your private life with, who give you input, who you spend your time with, and who provide support (or drag you down).

A strong inner circle is the fast track to disrupting Victim Habits. Why? Because these people have the most access to you, and the most influence on you. Show me your inner circle and I'll show you your values, your priorities and your habits. If you've got kids, you already know this. What are we always telling our kids? There are certain kids we don't want them hanging out with; those other kids we've deemed the "bad seeds." Why? Because of their influence.

Never underestimate the impacts of a bad inner circle. When you look at people who are not doing so well in life or making some really wrong turns, check out their inner circle. You'll get a few "a-ha" moments that reveal why things aren't going so well. So as you're evaluating your own inner circle, ask the question: Is your inner circle dragging you down? Is there someone in the circle who just really isn't adding anything? If so, it's time to clean house.

When you're moving out of Victim Habits, the move to rebuild your inner circle is a great disruptor because it gets the Habit-supporters out of your circle of influence. One of my favorite leadership influencers, Dr. John Maxwell, outlined five traits to look for when building your inner circle.[30] Take a look at these traits, and as you consider each member of your current inner circle, ask if they possess these characteristics:

- *Honesty and Character.* Does this inner circle member display exemplary character in everything they do?
- *Diverse Perspective.* Do they bring diverse yet complimentary perspectives to the table? These are different ways of thinking

about things and diverse perspectives are good to challenge you and your thinking.

- *Reliable Strategist.* Can this person be trusted to help you execute a chosen strategy? Are they supportive of your move to leave unproductive Victim Habits behind and implement healthier, more productive habits? Do they have the necessary influence and skill to help you in this way?
- *Adds Value.* Does this person have unique skills and expertise that will add value to you? Can you clearly articulate the value that they will add?
- *Emotional Intelligence.* Do they have the ability to positively impact other members of your inner circle even when they don't always agree?

Your inner circle is critical to your success. If you hang out with someone who delights in gossip, is critical of others and generally not in service to others, you'll find yourself falling deeper into the Victim Habits, not leaving them behind. Your inner circle re-do is about keeping you moving forward.

Great inner circle members won't let you wallow in misery. While they may be empathetic and compassionate, their compassion is *constructive.* They remind you to be your best self and they help you look forward and focus on your dreams, on rising above the fray. It's worth the time and effort to rebuild your inner circle to a support system that propels you ahead. And when you are moving forward, you create more space for your kids, for your loved ones and most importantly for yourself.

## Disruptor #5: Practice Gentleness

At the core of many Victim Habits is a critical, harsh spirit. You may find yourself pointing the critical stun-gun of unkindness toward others, yet most often you turn it on yourself. The harsh spirit typically shows up in the "Playing Small" Habit, the "Get Them, Before They Get You" Habit and the "Blame-Game" Habit. Occasionally we see it in the "Self-Imposed Helplessness" Habit, where the inner self-talk says something like, "Of course you can't do this, you're not smart enough..." But wherever it shows up, the practice of gentleness with yourself and others is a sure-fire way to interrupt the pattern of a Victim Habit.

We've all seen people in public places loudly communicating their displeasure with service at a restaurant, or other critical statements made in harsh, unkind ways. When we've been wronged deeply, we can walk around with a psychological sunburn that shows up in defensiveness and harsh treatment of ourselves and others.

I love the wisdom writings of King Solomon: "*A gentle answer turns away wrath, but a harsh answer stirs up anger.*"[31] Have you ever seen someone respond to an angry outburst (from you, a child, a spouse, or a co-worker) with quiet, kind words? It's really hard for the angry person to carry on. The gentle response truly does "turn away wrath." It diffuses conflict.

On the flip side, what happens when someone communicates in an irritated or angry way, and the people around them don't have gentleness on their minds? This is how shouting matches start and ugly confrontations start—because we are wired to *mirror* each other. This is attributable to the "mirror neurons" in our brains. These are the tools the brain engages when we show sympathy toward others.

I love to observe the mirroring effect during conversations with others. If I cross my legs, the other person crosses their legs. If I lean on the wall, the other person leans on the wall; all unnoticed while we are deep in cordial and sympathetic conversation. As a mediator, I would very intentionally sit in a very open, welcoming manner to induce mirroring by angry parties in the room. As I sat with my arms relaxed and open, draped on the arms of my chair, it was only seconds before the mirroring began, and the angry others started to calm down. If someone begins to raise their voice at you, listen quietly, and when it's time, respond in quiet, hushed tones and watch the de-escalation happen before your eyes.

Gentleness is the outward manifestation of a *grace* mindset. Grace is undeserved kindness. It's giving someone what they *need* instead of what they deserve. You may not have learned nor mastered the concept of grace, and that's OK. Now that you know what grace is, you can behave your way to gentleness through the conscious choice to give yourself and others what you/they *need*, regardless of whether or not you believe it is deserved.

The beauty of practicing gentleness and extending grace to yourself is that you don't need to believe you *deserve* acts of kindness to get started. Knowing that you *need* kindness and self-care is enough to get you going. For example, if you're in the Victim Habit of "Get Them, Before They Get You," you're likely critical of those around you, as a defense mechanism to push them away before they get too close. You may have convinced yourself that you don't "deserve" to have close, caring relationships and thus, you turn away all those who try to love on you.

But you know darned well that everyone, including you, *needs* to have the love and support of others in order to move forward to life's next assignment. So knowing this is a *need*, recognize that giving yourself permission to enjoy a close, supportive friendship is an expression of self-grace—providing yourself what you need, even if it's undeserved. This form of gentleness now becomes a chosen behavior, something to act upon, regardless of how deserving you feel.

Then there is your self-talk. Do you call yourself names like "stupid," "idiot," or other degrading titles? Do you criticize yourself? Focus your awareness on these habits this week, and stop in the moment to practice gentleness. What is the gentle response to the degrading name-calling? "No, I'm not stupid. In fact, I'm thankful for my intelligence and resourcefulness..." you might quietly say out loud. What is the gentle response to your own harsh criticisms? Perhaps it's pointing out the progress (remember your "Magic Moments" from priming) and identifying the next step you can take today to move toward your goal.

Another marvelous consequence of practicing gentleness is the *persuasive effect*. The gentle giants in leadership are usually the most persuasive. After all, when a leader guards their words, extends kindness and thoughtful conversation toward others, people listen. They are persuasive and others are attracted to them.

Practicing gentleness with yourself is a form of self-leadership. The persuasive effect of gentleness is an incredibly effective tool. You may not believe you deserve great things today, but through consistent gentleness you'll persuade your mind to reconsider.

## Disruptor #6: Leverage Redemptive Pain

Redemptive pain is the highest, best use of pain. When we allow our pain to become redemptive, it means we leverage it to help (redeem) others. The old adage, "It takes one to know one..." is so true. When you've gone through pain and suffering—particularly the kind of suffering that's through no fault of your own—you become uniquely positioned to help others through similar circumstances.

Remember C.S. Lewis and his journey through grief after the loss of his wife, Joy? Lewis leveraged that pain through his writings and release of *A Grief Observed* and other books after Joy's death. Redemption is the act of exchanging or releasing something. Redemptive pain is the converting or releasing of pain into something worthwhile. Leveraging redemptive pain is finding purpose in the pain to restore someone else.

Your pain and the life lessons that came from it are useful tools to help others suffering with the same problems. Viewing your pain as a tool to help others will disrupt a Victim Habit in short order, because redemptive pain moves you forward, into the service of others. After all, who better to help a woman going through a late-in-life divorce than another woman who's been through it? Who better to comfort a person who just got a breast cancer diagnosis than someone who's experienced the same thing?

Another factor in leveraging redemptive pain is *forgiveness*. When we've suffered harm, unforgiveness of the offender can block our ability to help others who are facing what we've faced. Bitterness and serving others are not mutually exclusive, but the ability to *effectively* help someone else is heavily impacted. Bitterness and unforgiveness rob you of your focus and your energy. Because this is such an important (and multifaceted) subject, I've given forgiveness its own chapter. We'll discuss it in depth in Chapter 10.

# 10

# The Forgiveness Factor

**Forgiving is a journey; the deeper
the wound, the longer the journey.**

*Lewis B. Smedes, The Art of Forgiving*

Forgiveness is the great liberator and the greatest disruptor of Victim Habits. So often we confuse the idea of forgiving with the concept of *exoneration,* even though the two are radically different. Exoneration is the act of absolving someone from blame; releasing them from a duty or an obligation. Forgiveness is not at all about the perpetrator, nor does it seek to shield a wrongdoer from the consequences of their actions. Forgiveness is not about being weak. It's not about being a Caspar Milquetoast. It's not about allowing people to treat you badly, excusing them for it and letting them walk all over you again and again.

To the contrary, forgiveness is an amazing *gift* you give to yourself—a freeing of your soul. When you choose to live in a state of unforgiveness, you take on a job you were never meant to have. You become a carrier and a storage house for *resentment and bitterness.* Forgiveness is all about untying the knots of bitterness and pain in your heart. Despite deep wounds, the act of forgiving is a series of conscious choices made over time—choices which are essential to making the shift from victim to your true self.

## The Consequences of Unforgiveness

Resentment and bitterness are like a cancer that grows inside, especially when fed a steady diet of unforgiveness. Pay attention to these two toxins, because they fester and spill out into your *entire life* if you allow them to grow. Unforgiveness changes who you are and affects how you treat people, not just the offender. Remaining in a state of unforgiveness means you are not allowing healing to occur. And that means you've been damaged from the inside out, and you stay damaged.

The phrase "hurting people hurt people" is so true about the person who hasn't learned the art of forgiveness. Unforgiveness manifests itself as inflicting pain on the people around us. It shows up in the perpetually angry spouse or parent, boiling over into verbal and physical abuse of children and life partners. It shows up in the alcoholic or the addict; the attempt to medicate and mask the pain of past hurts, instead of doing the raw and the real work of forgiving the wrongdoer. It shows up in the business owner who can't seem to keep a commitment or who fears venturing to the next level out of fear of being burned again.

And the most untenable consequence of unforgiveness? In my opinion, it's the continued giving away of your precious energy and life potential to your perpetrator. That's right. When you refuse forgiveness, you piss away your most valuable resource: You. You continue to hand yourself over to your wrongdoer. You continue to give away your power, your time, your focus and your energy to that which is in the past—at the expense of your future and of those around you.

I vividly remember a law client, Jennifer, whose grip on unforgiveness poisoned every relationship in her life and it came at a high cost. Jennifer was a beautiful woman in her mid-30's, and a single mom of twin girls. The twins' father was Jennifer's long-time boyfriend John. John and Jennifer split up when the girls were three, after Jennifer discovered that John had been cheating on her.

What was so striking about Jennifer was her absolute hatred for John. John's betrayal consumed Jennifer. Her entire focus was on her hatred for John and it was holding up her career. Jennifer was super bright, super talented, and super articulate. In the year after having the twins, she started a career in real estate and for a newcomer, she was doing really well.

Then the breakup happened and Jennifer's real estate deals started drying up. Jennifer became so obsessed with her resentment of John that it started to cloud everything. In the months that followed, Jennifer fought with John about everything, and she was on high-alert, watching and waiting for John to make a mistake of any kind. We had worked out a custody and visitation plan for Jennifer and John and the court ordered it. After explaining to Jennifer that there really was no reason for the court to limit John's time with the children, Jennifer grudgingly agreed to the visitation plan.

Right after the court ordered the visitation schedule, Jennifer started calling my office several times a day to report on John and why he was such a horrible person, undeserving of having a relationship with his daughters. It became exhausting wading through Jennifer's "concerns," most of which arose out of a bitter, critical filter that Jennifer put on everything John-related.

One afternoon I received a video Jennifer had made and sent to my paralegal, requesting that I view it. Jennifer stated that the video proved her daughters were emotionally traumatized at the thought of having to spend time with John. Hmmm, I thought, they were three years old...how could that be? I opened the video on my computer.

Jennifer was in the driver's seat of her car, with the twin girls in the back seat, each in their safety seats. To my horror, this is what I saw:

Jennifer: Ok girls, we're driving to daddy's house.

Twins: [Smiling]

Jennifer: I know that Daddy's house isn't as nice as Mommy's house and you won't have any of the toys you like there. But that's OK; you can have your favorite toys when you come home.

Twins: We won't have toys at Daddy's?

Jennifer: Not really. That's because Daddy doesn't care about toys.

Twins: We want our toys, Mommy!

Jennifer: I know, you'll miss your toys. But you know what I'll miss? I'll miss you both, really bad. Like you'll miss your toys. I'll be at home all by myself while you're at Daddy's, but that's OK. You won't have your toys or your nice beds at Daddy's, or me. But don't worry, it won't be forever.

Twins: I don't want to go to Daddy's! [Starting to cry...]

Jennifer: [Smiling into the camera...] Oh but you *have to go* to Daddy's.

Twins:     [Getting more upset, panicked] Why?! Why do we have to go?

Jennifer:  Because Daddy doesn't care about Mommy being sad and all alone and he doesn't care about your toys—but he's *making me* take you there.

Twins:     [Crying, getting very distressed...] We don't want to go to Daddy's! We want to stay with you, Mommy!

Jennifer:  [Smirking into the camera...] You don't want to go? You don't want to leave Mommy all by herself and sad?

Twins:     [Crying, getting hysterical...] No! No! We want to go home. We want to be with Mommy!

Jennifer:  [Smirking into the camera even more...] Ok girls, don't worry. I'll take you home. You can't go to Daddy's like this, you're too upset. I'll tell Daddy you don't want to go today.

Jennifer went on to tell my paralegal that she cancelled the visit and told John the girls were traumatized and she wasn't going to put them through a visit with him. This is the kind of stuff that parental alienation is made of and I told Jennifer so. This is the kind of behavior that causes courts to get sideways with a bitter parent. In the end, Jennifer refused to heed our advice and kept allowing her anger and bitterness toward John to lead her around by the nose and emotionally harm her little girls in the process. The judge in her family law case was not understanding, and as a result, Jennifer's time with the twins was *reduced* while John's time was *increased*.

Jennifer would repeatedly exclaim, "I hate him *so much!*" when referring to John. Her beautiful face would morph into an ugly, contorted version of Jennifer, with stress lines and hard, cold eyes. The bitterness grew so large in Jennifer that I was unable to help her. I eventually had to let her go as a client, while urging her to seek help from a therapist to sort out her anger.

Last I heard, Jennifer had blown up nearly every personal and professional relationship she had. She became known for her hostility and anger toward everyone. Jennifer's income dwindled to nothing and the financial stress became nearly unbearable. Jennifer told the judge she could not work because of what John had done to her, but the judge wasn't buying it and refused to increase her child support. The judge gave Jennifer the admonition I had repeatedly warned was coming: "You have the ability to work—so quit trying to punish the father of your children and focus on getting on with your life!"

Jennifer just wasn't interested in the "getting on with life" idea. She was too busy pouring the best of herself back into her "perpetrator" and she's paid a high price for unforgiveness.

Others most certainly feel the consequences of our refusal to embrace forgiveness. Who are affected most? Those who depend on you the most:

- Your children
- Your spouse
- Your best friends
- Your employees
- Your clients or customers

Like Jennifer, you may have been victimized. But there is no need to keep giving the wrongdoer your power, and allowing the most important people in your life to become resentment's collateral damage. The crime and the wrongdoer certainly don't deserve your good energy—it's like throwing good money after bad. Unforgiveness means you retain bitterness and resentment. That's a life sentence—not for the wrongdoer—but for *you* and your loved ones.

I have stood as the neutral observer in thousands of disputes—as the mediator—looking in from the outside. In that role I've witnessed *so many* talented people who've turned their backs on what "could be." They abandoned what they had to develop and to give because they allowed the pain and resentment of an unforgiven wrong to dominate their focus.

Anger, unforgiveness and resentment just get in the way. You've been put here on this earth for a multitude of reasons; the foremost of which is to bless others with your unique skills and talents. But how do you move from resentment and bitterness to a state of forgiveness? By taking one small, courageous step at a time.

## Who We Forgive

This business of forgiving isn't applicable to everyone, that's for sure. Forgiveness is a well-thought-out, deliberate act—a choice. There are a lot of people who do stupid things, often without realizing it, and we just overlook it or excuse it.

The things in life that are in the "just overlook it" category are not the serious things we're talking about here. The serious business of forgiveness is really applicable to four types of people: Those we *blame*, those who *don't say they're sorry, ourselves*, and *God*.

**Forgiving Those We Blame.** Who is it that you actually *blame* for the pain, the damage that you incurred? Those we blame are the target of our resentment. This is perhaps the most obvious target for your forgiveness. After all, it's easy to point out who we feel is to blame for the wrongdoing we have suffered.

**Forgiving Those Who Don't Say They're Sorry.** This takes forgiveness up a level. Someone you blame for your pain may be remorseful, and may even apologize. Those folks at least make the idea of forgiveness more palatable, because humility and ownership of wrongdoing is an instant heart softener.

When someone is to blame for your pain and they're never sorry...well, that becomes one tough pill to swallow. I'll bet you can think of loads of objections to extending forgiveness to a person with no remorse. Let's look at a few of the obvious:

*Objection #1—"They don't deserve to be forgiven if they're not sorry!"* Of course they don't *deserve* to be forgiven. If they deserved forgiveness, you'd just excuse them and overlook the wrong. But that's not forgiving.

*Objection #2—"It's too hard to forgive someone who's not sorry."* Wait, wait, wait a minute! This objection is the result of a loss of focus. Remember, forgiveness is *your* path to *your* healing. When you feel the burn of a wrongdoer's lack of remorse, it's not your job to make them wake up and see the light. Your job is to heal yourself, and stop giving that joker the best parts of you. Remember what unforgiveness does *to you* and count the cost.

*Objection #3—"If I forgive this person, they're likely to do it again."* This objection is about wanting to stop unjust acts of a perpetrator. The reality is, neither my forgiveness nor yours is the "fix." The fix lies in the work the wrongdoer must do for him or herself, to get to the root of why that person does harmful things.

The good news is, you aren't responsible for making sure the wrongdoer is stopped from working another injustice on someone else. While it is a noble thought, it is not your job. One of my favorite Bible verses says, "...do not take revenge, my dear friends, but leave room for God's wrath, for it is written: 'It is mine to avenge; I will repay,' says the Lord."[32] This is such a comfort to me, because what I know is God, karma, the Universe or whatever you may call it, is a much better "avenger" than I could ever be.

*Objection #4—"I don't want them back in my life to hurt me all over again."* That's the old "forgive and forget" fallacy. Don't confuse forgiving with welcoming them back to the relationship, or the fold. The kind of forgiveness I'm encouraging you to embrace is an act that is truly an *inside job.*

A lot of people think forgiveness is an outward act of saying to the wrongdoer, "That's OK. I'm not holding it against you anymore, I'm not mad anymore, all is forgotten and put in the past." That post-forgiveness piece, when extended to the wrongdoer, is truly an extension of both grace and an invitation to reconciliation. That's next-level stuff that ultimately you may or may not want to do.

Forgiveness sometimes results in a message to the wrongdoer that you have extended forgiveness to them. This message is often a natural byproduct, because your forgiveness is revealed in how you *behave* toward the person who hurt you. But the real act of forgiv-ing—the inside job—requires nothing more than a *desire* to be rid of your resentment.

Whether forgiveness becomes a gift to the wrongdoer is not dependent upon you. This is the interesting aspect of forgiveness. No one can truly *receive* forgiveness until they own their wrongful act and are sorry for it. But that doesn't mean you can't forgive your wrongdoer if they aren't sorry; they just won't get the benefit of the forgiveness until they can truly *"receive"* it.

**Forgiving Ourselves.** Why would forgiving yourself be a consid-eration when you've been victimized in one way or another? For all the people I've represented and counseled over the years, it was the rare circumstance where a victim didn't *also* blame themselves for what happened to them. Victims frequently blame *only themselves* for their suffering. Remember the victim blaming and shaming phenomenon discussed in Chapter One? This cultural shame-game has very real impacts. Forgiving *yourself* as part of the forgiveness process should never be overlooked. If you don't forgive yourself, you risk living in a perpetual state of self-hatred.

So, what is it you forgive yourself for? First, you forgive yourself for what you *did*, not for *who you are*. This is about self-acceptance and rejecting self-judgment and self-loathing. Let's say you went on a spending spree without checking your bank balances, and you overdrafted your account. As a result, you incurred overdraft fees that you can't really afford. Then, your spouse learns of the error, and gets really upset. And of course, you're embarrassed.

If you told me that what you did was pretty stupid (going on a spending spree without knowing whether there's dough in the bank to cover it), I'd probably agree with you. But I wouldn't agree that *you* were stupid. For crying out loud, even true-blue rocket scientists do things like that now and again.

The point is, you forgive yourself for *the act*, without assassinating your character. This is about forgiving yourself for *specific things* you did. Please! Don't generalize and call yourself an utter failure. That leads you right back to character assassination and there's no value in that. Instead of putting yourself down, ask two questions:

(1) "What happened?" and
(2) "What am I going to do differently, going forward?"

These two questions are productive. They're the path to learning from your mistake, forgiving yourself for the specific thing you did, and moving on. When you take the time to do this, you'll not miss the lesson that failures bring...they're rich! By the way, life has a way of presenting the same "lessons" again and again, until we decide to truly learn those lessons (so save time and start asking the right questions, right now).

**Forgiving God.** Yes, I'm going there. I recognize that for many people this is a touchy subject. But I'll risk "going there" because I believe (and know) that it's a subject worth exploring.

In one of the greatest writings on forgiveness, *The Art of Forgiving*, Dr. Lewis B. Smedes (a renowned theologian and professor at Fuller Theological Seminary in Pasadena, California) tackled the subject of anger at God in the face of suffering. Smedes offered compelling and thought-provoking reasons why we should consider forgiving God.[33] Of course, this argument presumes that you believe in God, and I'll presume that here, too. My presumption is because whether you call God "God" or you refer to "the Universe" or "karma" or whatever, I haven't run across a single soul that hasn't questioned the "why" of suffering.

I believe at the heart of every human, there is a primal understanding that someone, or at least something larger that the human race, is at the helm. And besides, you can't run around being mad at God (or whatever you call Her) forever. Just like giving away your good, productive energy to a perpetrator, being mad at the world is just as unproductive (for differing reasons).

Another compelling read is C.S. Lewis' *The Problem of Pain*. As you know from the earlier story of Lewis and the loss of his wife Joy, Lewis was well acquainted with pain and suffering. In *The Problem of Pain,* Lewis suggests that pain is God's megaphone, which God uses to get the attention of a deaf world. In other words, God uses pain to shake us up and get us to listen to Him.[34]

The bottom line is: Bad things happen to good people. It's not surprising that we blame God—that's normal. If you're a person of faith, remember that God's shoulders are big enough to take our blame and our anger. If you're not a person of faith, I encourage you to investigate and find that spiritual connection (because when you do, you'll be astounded by the increased richness of life). When you do get angry at God, it's worth the effort to extend the idea of forgiveness God's way. Through that process, you'll likely make some discoveries about yourself and your calling; discoveries you'd never have known had God not yelled through the megaphone.

## The Process of Forgiving

Here's where the rubber meets the road. Below is a four-step process for effective forgiveness. It may surprise you, depending on what your assumptions have been about forgiving someone. For the person who's been wronged, this is a process that leads to release; the freedom of your soul. Ready? Let's begin.

### Step 1: Humanize the Wrongdoer

Humanizing the wrongdoer makes it easier to start down the road of forgiveness. Rediscovering the humanity of the person who hurt you so badly softens your heart, and a soft heart opens you up to *healing*. Remember, this is about *you*. Moving forward in life with a soft heart causes you to be much more open and receptive to others, allowing deep, meaningful relationships to form. Living with a soft, open heart allows you to see and hear new opportunities for personal growth that you cannot see when your heart is hard and your eyes are closed.

How have you been thinking about the person who wronged you? Have you put labels on that person? It's so easy to label the wrongdoer in a way that removes his or her *humanity*.

To the husband whose wife was unfaithful, she easily becomes the cheater, the slut, the whore. To the CEO whose bookkeeper embezzled money from the company, that employee becomes the thief, the con artist, the crook. To the woman whose car was broken into at the mall, that person becomes the crackhead, the thug, the loser. These labels allow us to become hardened against the wrongdoer—a natural reaction to pain. After all, when you harden your heart against someone, it feels like a protective shell to ward off further vulnerabilities.

But what happens when you allow yourself to rediscover the humanity of the person who hurt you so badly? A beautiful transition happens. When you cast off the labels, you begin to see your own humanity in the transgressor.

One of the great gifts of mediating disputes for people is what I get to observe. People tend to reveal the rawest form of themselves when directly addressing conflict and those they blame for their pain. At the close of each mediation case, I'll ask each party (privately) what they felt was the hardest part of the mediation process. Nine times out of ten, they tell me it was the thought of walking into my office and seeing the other person face-to-face. Nine times out of ten, they were most impacted by coming face-to-face with the "wrongdoer," by looking them in the eyes and rediscovering how very human they are.

What was happening in those moments? Connection and recognition that we all make mistakes. Rediscovering the humanity of he who caused you so much pain and damage allows you to take your own inventory. It brings to the surface those moments in life when you caused pain to others and the part (if any) you may have played in the conflict. Most of all, it allows you to lay down the burdens of hatred and bitterness and finally grant *yourself* peace. Perhaps Dr. Smedes said it best: "As we start on the miracle of forgiving, we begin to see our enemy through a cleaner lens, less smudged by hate."[35]

## Step 2: Make a Choice to Give Up on Vengeance

Everyone has a sequence of behaviors they exhibit in response to conflict. Your conflict sequence may be to fight back, analyze what happened, deny what happened, grieve your losses. Your spouse's sequence might be to first deeply analyze what happened, grieve the loss, then launch a lifetime effort to get even. Mine happens to be analyze what happened (briefly), strategize how to get even, then fight back tooth and nail (no doubt, that inner justice warrior takes the reigns, no surprise for us lawyer-types). Understanding your own conflict sequence helps you to recognize what's going on, and to choose a different path that serves you better.

For most people, at some point in the conflict sequence there's a preoccupation with the right to get even. When you decide to embark on the journey of forgiveness, you must give up that right. Waiving the right to excise revenge can be a bitter pill to swallow—at first. It's natural to want to make the other person "pay" and feel as much pain as you felt. After all, hurting people hurt people.

But giving up on vengeance is not giving up on justice. Vengeance/revenge is a pleasure-seeking endeavor. When you seek revenge, you're chasing the pleasure of seeing the wrongdoer get back the kind of hurt they dished out, and then some. Justice, on the other hand, happens when the wrongdoer pays a fair penalty for his bad act. Much of the time, "justice" fails to deliver any feeling of pleasure or resolution to the person who was wronged.

So why waive the "right" to get even? Because giving up this right also *frees you* from a whole lot of sideways energy. It's a heavy burden. When you live life on a mission to mete out revenge, it's like trying to run a marathon with a one hundred pound rucksack on your back. You may finish the race but you'll be last, beat up and exhausted, as you cross the finish line.

## Step 3: Choose New Feelings About
## the Person You're Forgiving

This is about moving from a place of hate to a place of grace. And it only comes *after* we rediscover our enemy's *humanity* and *after* we give up our right to "get even." Feeling differently about a wrongdoer will never come before the first two steps in the forgiveness process. It's the humanity piece that enables you to revise your feelings toward the person you're forgiving. This is especially true for betrayals that involve passions of the heart, greed and insecurities.

Changing your feelings is really about choosing. Yes, you most certainly can *choose* how you feel about another person. When you've been harmed, transforming your feelings about the wrongdoer starts with acknowledging their humanity while *deciding* to discontinue your hidden wish for "karma" or God or the universe to get revenge on them.

Next, shift your focus and watch your feelings shift. That's what happened in most of my mediation cases, when those feuding parties came face-to-face with each other in my office. Their focus shifted from the sterile, non-human labels they gave each other, to the humanity staring them back in the face. The more the feuding parties focused on each other's humanity, the more their feelings toward each other shifted.

To aid in the shift, make a list of all the roles the wrongdoer plays, and humanize them (if you don't know them well, make an educated guess). Take the embezzler for example. I had this happen to me a number of years ago. I discovered that one of my most trusted employees had been embezzling small amounts of money over the course of several years, and boy was I mad. I had trusted this employee (let's call her Monica) and I felt betrayed. For awhile I would refer to Monica as "sticky-fingers." Although Monica was gone and I recovered most of what she had stolen, I was still mad as a wet hen.

When I decided to revise my feelings toward Monica, I set myself free and opened the door to forgiveness. Instead of calling her sticky-fingers, I thought about Monica's roles in life. She was a mother of four children and a wife in a very sad marriage where her husband had repeatedly been unfaithful. Monica was a daughter to a mother who never accepted her—who never told Monica that she loved her—and who never gave Monica a compliment. Monica was a college graduate, having obtained her degree as a single mother and with no family support. Monica was a talented legal professional who was a perfectionist and very hard on herself.

The more I thought about Monica's *humanity*, the more I realized how desperate she was to feel *significant* in this world. Monica's conduct was criminal, but her humanity was relatable. The pain I suffered as a result of Monica's wrongful conduct paled in comparison to the rejection she experienced throughout her life. My bitterness would not make Monica better. My bitterness diluted my focus on the important things in life that matter.

I did not excuse what Monica did, but I did choose to think of her differently. I made a conscious choice to change my feelings toward Monica, from anger and resentment to feelings of hope and empathy. In the process of forgiving Monica, I was able to sincerely pray that she find the courage to face her demons that drove her behavior, and discover that she didn't need to lie, cheat and steal her way to a life of significance (which will never happen). As a result of forgiving Monica, I was able to genuinely wish her well.

## Step 4: Rinse and Repeat

You noticed that the steps laid out here are called the *process* of forgiveness, right? It is very much a process, and not a one-time event. That's where the Rinse and Repeat aspect comes in. To truly forgive a wrongdoer, you'll do it more than one time. It's like scrubbing a deep stain off a white t-shirt. It usually takes a few washes and some deep soaking in bleach to lift it out.

Some of this forgiveness business is tough stuff and requires patience with yourself. They don't teach us how to embark on the path to healing forgiveness in school. But I assure you it's worth it. Miracles truly do happen when you trust and follow the process.

Your feelings of resentment, anger, pain and bitterness don't go away overnight. They go away one choice to refocus at a time. One of the best stories on this Rinse and Repeat concept is in the scriptures—this is my last Bible story for you and it's a goodie. In the Book of Matthew, the apostle Peter approached Jesus on the topic of forgiveness. Peter no doubt was struggling with the idea of forgiving someone, especially when his feelings told him otherwise and the wrongdoer kept doing wrong. Peter asked Jesus (paraphrased), "...so Jesus, exactly how many times do I need to forgive this joker, when he keeps doing me wrong? Seven times? Or what?" The answer was profound. Jesus replied, "No Pete, not seven times. More like 70 times 7..."[36]

What Jesus was telling Peter was, we forgive as many times as it takes. The phrase "70 times 7" was meant to signify boundlessness, infinity, whatever it takes. The message was, *forgive as often as you need to!* I think Jesus was trying to help Peter understand that the forgiving is for the *forgiver*.

You can just feel the tension Peter was experiencing over this. He was thinking about a wrongdoer who just didn't get it; who just kept being a bad apple. Yet Jesus was telling him to be the bigger person and forgive over and over. But did you notice what Jesus did *not* tell Peter to do? The answer lies in what forgiveness is *not*:

- *Forgiveness Is Not a Substitute for Common Sense.* You don't throw common sense out the window just because you've forgiven someone. This is where the ridiculousness of the old phrase "forgive and forget" is exposed. Remember the difference between forgiveness and justice? They're in two separate categories: Forgiving is something the offended *does.* Your forgiveness stands alone. It's independent of anything the wrongdoer has done. Justice is a fair penalty, a consequence to be paid by the offender for what they have done.

Sometimes we think forgiveness means restoring an offender back to their former position in a relationship, in a job, in a position of influence. To the contrary, restoring a wrongdoer to their former position is very much dependent on the offender's conduct and society's common sense. Remember Monica, my embezzling former employee? Even though I've forgiven Monica, common sense says it would be foolish to allow her to come back to work for me, especially in a position where she'd have access to money.

• ***Forgiveness Is Not Re-unification with the Wrongdoer.*** We often confuse the word "reconciliation" for reunion. Reconciliation is the ***result*** of forgiveness. Reconciliation may occur, like welcoming a person back into a group of people we try to care about (like welcoming a wrong-doing family member back to the annual family picnic, or putting them back on your Christmas card list.) Or it might look like continuing to socialize in the same *external* circles in which you frequent.

But forgiveness does not mean you necessarily welcome a wrongdoer into your inner circle; that group of family and friends with whom you have special, intimate, trusting relationships. Reconciliation through forgiveness can be (and most often is) a one-sided event. I can forgive you even if you are not sorry, and refuse to own your part of the wrongdoing.

Remember, you *don't need the wrongdoer to do, or own, anything in order for you to forgive him.*

To *restore* the relationship, to be re-united...well that's a much different story. True reunion with a wrongdoer only happens when the wrongdoer is honestly *sorry* for what he did and can be *trusted* to not wrong you again. There's a lot of work to be done for reunion after forgiveness to occur, and a lot of common sense to be applied. Forgiveness is something that happens in *your* heart, but it may not be in the best interest of anyone involved for a reunion to occur.

- *Forgiveness Is Not About Letting the Bad Conduct Happen Again, nor Is It About Forgetting What Happened.* Back to common sense! Consider Jackson, a young man who was physically abused by his father—an angry alcoholic—throughout his childhood. As an adult, would it be OK for Jackson to allow his children to be around his abusive father, and potentially allow it to happen all over again? Of course not.

  You have a memory for a reason. In forgiving, you do not choose to turn a blind eye to reality. Forgiveness combined with our memory allows us to move forward in peace, bathed in wisdom. Knowing what you now know about a wrongdoer, you can let go of anger and resentment while being mindful of what the offender is capable of doing, and act accordingly.

Forgiveness is truly as much an art as it is the gift of freedom. To help you put the process of forgiveness into action, I've created a *Forgiveness Worksheet* bonus in Appendix B at the end of this book. I've also created a digital version for you on VictimIsNotYourName.com, where you can use the Worksheet as often as you like. I encourage you to think about the things in your life that you hold bitterness and resentment over, and list them. Then one by one, complete a *Forgive-ness Worksheet* for each issue, and dive into the process of forgiving those you blame.

As you do the good, liberating work of forgiveness, you'll notice that each stage of the process is work you do *internally*. Forgiveness is totally separate and apart from the offender. None of it is *dependent* upon what the offender does or does not do. How freeing it is to understand that forgiveness is an *inside job*. Your wrongdoer holds no power over you. My hope for you is that you'll grab on tight to the power of forgiveness, and be free from the pain that glues you to those bruised moments in your past.

# PART FOUR
## LET'S GET THIS PARTY STARTED
-------------------------------------------------

# 11

# The Invitation
of a Lifetime

**As soon as healing takes place,
go out and heal somebody else.**

*Maya Angelou*

You've done it! You've taken a huge step by diving into the ideas presented here. While I'm no therapist or psychology expert, I have been gifted with seeing so much in others that they cannot see in the midst of their woundedness. I invite you to take some calculated time to "go deeper" and reflect on the ideas and tools in this book. Take some time to plan your foray into the deep, healing waters. Living in the shallows isn't where it's at. Schedule time to go back and review, re-read, contemplate and ultimately, *implement*.

A key to moving forward is to *celebrate* every small win along the way. I invite you to close this book and get your celebration groove on. Celebrate the fact that you finished this book. Celebrate your bravery to consider the ideas and dare to apply them to yourself *right now*. These small wins are the building blocks of a huge, monumental win. It's rare that the "big win" is one event; rather, the "big win" is the sum total of all the small wins along the way...so *celebrate.*

As a child, I remember the two times a year my sister and I were allowed to take the beautiful antique china out of my mother's tall glass china cabinet. I'd ask mom if we could use those dishes more often, to which she'd reply, "No! That's the good china. It's only for *special* occasions." I always wondered why we had to wait for Thanksgiving and Christmas to use those pretty dishes. After all, those beautiful plates were right there, gathering dust and just waiting for us to take them out...all year long!

As an adult, I decided that life is now, and there's no reason to not use the good stuff. I believe the really *special* occasions are those in life where we stretch, grow and step into our true selves. Every advance, every gain along the way is indeed a *special* occasion—more than a Thanksgiving or Christmas holiday. Life is so much bigger and richer when you focus on your gains and celebrate regularly. So friend, pat yourself on the back and break out the good stuff. What are you waiting for?

## The Warrior's Payoff

Sometimes the gravity of life's challenges require us to go to war against those circumstances that leave us believing that we're damaged goods. You're a warrior and when you implement even one percent of the tactics provided in this book, you'll make major advancements. Taking the leap into the one percent isn't always easy, but the payoffs are larger than the victim life. You'll experience healing. And the best way to express your gratitude for your healing is to go out and heal others.

Let me remind you, dear one, that there's only one True You. Let not the world, nor its circumstances, tell you otherwise. Welcome to your new life, where you are a victim no more.

# Acknowledgments

This book reflects the power of my inner circle. Each member was a critical pillar in the raising of this work. They are my support beams and at times, the load-bearing walls. The voices of a million angels could not express how grateful I am for each one:

*My Groom, Greg Bennett*—*The consummate coach and cheerleader, the rock-steady voice of reason: "No, you cannot work seven days a week." "Don't be silly, of course it's good!" "No, the world does not already know this stuff." "Just write and let God take care of the rest." Thank you for never doubting, and ever listening to the manic flood of words. You are the most generous spirit I know; giving up a summer of surfing and eight months of downtime. Never grumbling or complaining. You are the definition of best friend. I am most grateful that you are my person—the one who understands what it means to be called, and the eternal impacts of answering that call.*

*Lil' Sis, Melinda Felton*—*My never-say-no sounding board. Thank you for the "sister-humor" and 24/7 availability to have your brain picked, and picked, and picked. Your deep empathy and love for people have inspired me to keep going. Thank you for letting me share a piece of your life in this book. Vulnerability is your strong suit.*

***Creative Director and All-Around Butt-Kicker, Jose Bono***—*Your endless patience and ability to see the big picture helped redirect my eyes to the prize (on more than a dozen occasions)...despite a few classic "melt-downs." Thank you for kicking me in the booty time and time again, and the non-stop reminders to get out of my own way. Chop wood, carry water. Your art, insights and hard work to super-charge the infrastructure of all we're doing in the law and at L3 are amazing.*

***Queen Copy Editor, Helen Ryan***—*Your skills kept this lawyer from complicating the message. Thank you for keeping it readable and reminding me that stories are the great connector.*

***Coach Debra Russell***—*You've shown me the path to a calm, centered state through conscious living. Thank you for bringing all the tools to bear during this writing process. With your help, I was able to master and orchestrate my strengths to work together for good.*

# Notes, References & Resources

Below I've listed relevant notes, references and resources used in each chapter of this book. Where you see "KAB Note," you'll find my comments and insights on the subject/resource. These resources are *also available online* at **VictimIsNotYourName. com**. There you can forward resource links to friends, family and co-workers, and more.

## Chapter 1: "Victim" is an Adjective—Not a Name

[1] Maria Konnikova, "Why Your Name Matters," The New Yorker (The New Yorker, June 19, 2017), https://www.newyorker.com/tech/annals-of-technology/why-your-name-matters.

[2] David Scott Yeager et al., "The Far-Reaching Effects of Believing People Can Change: Implicit Theories of Personality Shape Stress, Health, and Achievement During Adolescence," *Journal of Personality and Social Psychology*, 106, no. 6 (2014): pp. 867-884, https://doi.org/10.1037/a0036335.

[3] Art Markman, Ph.D., "The Danger of Labeling Others (or Yourself)," Psychology Today (psychologytoday.com, June 13, 2014), https://www.psychologytoday.com/us/blog/ulterior-motives/201406/the-danger-labeling-others-or-yourself.

[4] Ashley Crossman, "An Overview of Labeling Theory," ThoughtCo.com (December 30, 2018), https://www.thoughtco.com/labeling-theory-3026627.

[5] Judith E. Glaser, "The Neuroscience of Identity," Psychology Today (psychologytoday.com, July 17, 2019), https://www.psychologytoday.com/us/blog/conversational-intelligence/201907/the-neuroscience-identity.

[6] Meghan L. Meyer, Matthew D. Lieberman, "Why People Are Always Thinking About Themselves," Social Cognitive Neuroscience Laboratory, UCLA (reprinted from Massachusetts Institute of Technology, Journal of Cognitive Neuroscience, X:Y, pp. 1–8 doi:10.1162/jocn_a_01232), accessed November 10, 2019, https://www.scn.ucla.edu/pdf/Meyer(2018)JCN.pdf.

## Chapter 2: The Right to Call Yourself a Victim (For a Minute)

[7] DitchTheLabel.com, "Why do People Bully? The Scientific Reasons" (November 14, 2018), https://us.ditchthelabel.org/why-do-people-bully based on the 2018 Annual Bullying Survey where over 9,000 young people aged 12-20 were surveyed (with help from schools and colleges across the U.K.)—access the report here: https://www.ditchthelabel.org/research-papers/the-annual-bullying-survey-2018.

[8] Laura Niemi and Liane Young, "When and Why We See Victims as Responsible," *Personality and Social Psychology Bulletin* 42, no. 9 (November 2016): pp. 1227-1242, https://doi.org/10.1177/0146167216653933.

[9] Kayleigh Roberts, "The Psychology of Victim-Blaming: When people want to believe that the world is just, and that bad things won't happen to them, empathy can suffer," The Atlantic (Atlantic Media Company, October 5, 2016), https://www.theatlantic.com/science/archive/2016/10/the-psychology-of-victim-blaming/502661.

## Chapter 5: Good Grief and the Masquerade Bawl

[10] "Complicated Grief," Mayo Clinic (Mayo Foundation for Medical Education and Research, October 5, 2017), https://www.mayoclinic.org/diseases-conditions/complicated-grief/symptoms-causes/syc-20360374.

[11] N. W. Clerk, *A Grief Observed* (Greenwich, CT: Seabury Pr., 1963).

[12] Rick Warren, "You Don't Have to Be Happy All the Time—Daily Hope with Rick Warren—July 3, 2019," Crosswalk.com (Salem Web Network, June 26, 2019), https://www.crosswalk.com/devotionals/daily-hope-with-rick-warren/you-don-t-have-to-be-happy-all-the-time-daily-hope-with-rick-warren-july-3-2019.html.

## Chapter 6: The Price of Poker (Why a Victim Identity Doesn't Serve You Long-Term)

[13] Hebrews 11:1 NLT

[14] James 4:8 CSB

KAB Note: I love this super-relatable translation from *The Message* version of James 4:8, "Say a quiet 'yes' to God and he'll be there in no time. Quit dabbling in sin. Purify your inner life. Quit playing the field." Alrighty then!

[15] Friedrich Wilhelm Nietzsche, *Twilight of the Idols: or, How to Philosophise with the Hammer; The Anti-Christ; Notes to Zarathustra and Eternal Recurrence* (New York: Gordon Press, 1974).

## Chapter 7: Priming Yourself To Make The Shift

[16] Gay Hendricks, *The Big Leap: Conquer Your Hidden Fear and Take Life to the Next Level* (New York: HarperCollins, 2010))

[17] Stephen R. Covey, *The 7 Habits of Highly Effective People: Powerful Lessons in Personal Change* (New York: Simon & Schuster, 2013).

## Chapter 9: Six Paths To Utter Disruption

[18] KAB Note: *Hoarders* is the wildly a popular reality show on A&E Television Networks, LLC about "...Professionals [who] try to help people

who compulsively hoard possessions...", see https://www.aetv.com/shows/hoarders.

[19] Marie Kondo, *The Life-Changing Habit of Tidying Up: The Japanese Art of Decluttering and Organizing* (New York: Ten Speed Press/Crown Publishing Group 2014).

[20] Kondo, *The Life-Changing Habit.*

[21] Richard Merritt, "Study: Exercise Has Long-Lasting Effect on Depression," Duke Today, https://today.duke.edu/2000/09/exercise922.html.

[22] Rick Hanson, *Resilient: How to Grow an Unshakeable Core of Calm, Strength and Happiness* (Random House, 2018).

[23] "The Science of Positive Brain Change," Dr. Rick Hanson, https://www.rickhanson.net/the-science-of-positive-brain-change.

[24] KAB Note—**Brain vs. Mind:** Dr. Rick Hanson described the difference beautifully in a 2019 interview with Marie Forleo on her award-winning show, MarieTV. To watch the entire interview, go here https://www.marieforleo.com/2019/03/rick-hanson-inner-strength.

[25] Margaret Jaworski, "The Negativity Bias: Why the Bad Stuff Sticks and How to Overcome It," Psycom.net, (June 8, 2018), https://www.psycom.net/negativity-bias.

[26] Hanson, *Resilient,* p. 63.

[27] Viktor Emil. Frankl, *Man's Search for Meaning: An Introduction to Logotherapy* (Boston: Beacon Press, 1962).

[28] Frankl, *Man's Search,* p. 67.

[29] Ibid, p. 71.

[30] John Maxwell, "A Leader's Inner Circle," John Maxwell, June 11, 2011, https://www.johnmaxwell.com/blog/a-leaders-inner-circle.

[31] Proverbs 15:1 NIV

## Chapter 10: The Forgiveness Factor

[32] Romans 12:19 NIV

[33] Lewis B. Smedes, *The Art of Forgiving: When You Need to Forget and Don't Know How* (New York: Ballatine Books, 1997).

KAB Note: In my humble opinion, Dr. Smedes' research and teaching on forgiveness is the best ever. As a mediator, helping people for 30 years through legal and personal conflict, I have drawn on the wisdom presented in *The Art of Forgiving* for years.

[34] Clive S. Lewis, *The Problem of Pain* (New York, NY: Harper Collins, 2014).

[35] Smedes, *The Art of Forgiving*, p. 6.

[36] Matthew 18:21-22 MSG

# APPENDIX A

# Priming Checklist and Prep Sheet
## Priming Checklist—Daily Rituals (Morning)

☐ Breathing Quick-Starter—3 Minutes of Power
(Wake up, shift into a state of exhilaration!)
  ☐ Set 1: 30 inhales (arms up), 30 exhales (arms down).
  *Rest for 10 seconds, notice the energized sensation.*
  ☐ Set 2: 30 inhales (arms up), 30 exhales (arms down).
  Rest for 10 seconds, notice the energized sensation.
  ☐ Set 3: 30 inhales (arms up), 30 exhales (arms down).
  *Rest for 10 seconds, notice the energized sensation.*

☐ Mediation/Prayer—5 Minutes of Quiet Reflection, Mantra/Scripture Focus
  ☐ Mantra/Scripture for the Day:
  ☐ I'd like guidance on (prayer requests):
  ☐ In being quiet, the following ideas, revelations came to mind:

☐ Gratitude– 5 Minutes of Quiet Reflection, Mantra/Scripture Focus
  ☐ Three things/people I'm grateful for (say "Thank You" out loud):
  ☐ Magic Moments—Three positive things that happened in the last 24 hours that I feel good about:

### Priming Checklist—Daily Rituals (Evening)

☐   Breathe Into the Evening—2 Minutes to Wind-down
    ☐   Set 1:   Slow inhale through nose, hold for 5 seconds. Slow exhale through mouth.
          During exhale, think of something good that happened during the day, and say a prayer of thanks.
    ☐   Set 2:   Slow inhale through nose, hold for 5 seconds. Slow exhale through mouth.
          During exhale, think of something good that happened during the day, and say a prayer of thanks.
    ☐   Set 3:   Slow inhale through nose, hold for 5 seconds. Slow exhale through mouth.
          During exhale, think of something good that happened during the day, and say a prayer of thanks.

☐   Extend Gratitude—This evening, I told someone how much I appreciate them.

# Priming Prep Sheet
## Getting Clarity, Taking Action (30 Minutes)

Identity Questions

- **How have I been defining myself?**
  (Think about yourself in the third person. Imagine you're an outsider, an observer (the "Observer-You"). Observer-You is looking at you, seeing how you move about your days, and hearing the words you say to yourself.)

  a. Observer—You would describe me as:

  b. Based on what Observer-You is seeing, she/he would reasonably conclude that I believe the following things about myself:

- **What identity would make me feel great about myself?**

  a. If I were _____ (identity), I would feel hopeful about my future (list 2-4):

b.  The untrue, limiting beliefs I've been accepting about myself are:

c.  If I believed these things about myself (liberating beliefs), I'd feel free to experience an extraordinary life:

I am...

I can...

☐  I have decided to adopt the liberating beliefs about myself today (in place of the untrue, limiting beliefs).

"What Do I Want" Questions
*This is about getting clear about what you really want in life. Clarity about what fulfills you helps you discover your purpose. Taking the time to gain this clarity helps you shift your focus, helping you see your new future.*

1.  **What do I love?**

a.  Casting aside all of my fears, doubts, shame, anger, negative feelings, these 2-3 things feel meaningful to me:

b. I feel passionate about:

c. Assuming I cannot fail, who do I want to be?

2. **Knowing what I'm passionate about, and what makes me feel hopeful about the future, this is what I really want:**

3. **A remarkable life for me looks like this in the next 12 months (what I'll get, experience, get free from, do):**

   a. When those things in #3 above become true for me, the pay-offs will be:

   b. For those things in #3 to happen, this is what has to be true?

   c. I need to believe the following about myself for those things to happen:

   d. What is preventing me from making that remarkable life happen is:

e.  What needs to change right now to make it happen is:



f.  The actions I can take right now to change it are:



☐  I have calendared at least one action I will take this week to start making the changes I need to make my life remarkable over the next 6 to 12 months.

# APPENDIX B

# Forgiveness Worksheet

Prepare to Forgive—Identify The People I Blame

### Issue #1: I'm bitter/resentful about:

I blame the following people/persons for what happened:

If I harbor unforgiveness against this person, the consequences will be:

Who will be affected the most by my continued resentment, besides me?

### Issue #2: I'm bitter/resentful about:

I blame the following people/persons for what happened:

If I harbor unforgiveness against this person, the consequences will be:

Who will be affected the most by my continued resentment, besides me?

### Issue #3: I'm bitter/resentful about:

I blame the following people/persons for what happened:

If I harbor unforgiveness against this person, the consequences will be:

Who will be affected the most by my continued resentment, besides me?

**Issue #4: I'm bitter/resentful about:**

I blame the following people/persons for what happened:

If I harbor unforgiveness against this person, the consequences will be:

Who will be affected the most by my continued resentment, besides me?

**When I need to forgive *MYSELF*:**

Checklist of Important Reminders

☐ I'm being mindful that I forgive myself for *what I did,* not for who I am.

☐ In this process of forgiving myself, I'll *refrain* from assassinating my character. There is no value in character assassination.

Forgiving Myself for My Actions

**Issue #1:** I blame myself for the following thing(s) I did:

(a) What happened?

(b) What am I going to do differently, going forward?

If I fail to forgive myself, the consequences will be:

Who will be affected the most if I continue in unforgiveness, besides me?

**Issue #2:** I blame myself for the following thing(s) I did:

(a) What happened?

(b) What am I going to do differently, going forward?

If I fail to forgive myself, the consequences will be:

Who will be affected the most if I continue in unforgiveness, besides me?

Step 1—Humanize the Wrongdoers

### Wrongdoer #1: Impersonal Labels and Human Realities

Impersonal labels I have given this person while in a state of unforgiveness:

*(Examples: Cheat, liar, loser, slob...)*

Today I'll start thinking of this person in terms of their *humanity, describing them as*:

*(Examples: A mother of two young children whose husband is deployed; a man struggling with chronic pain; an elderly woman living alone and medicating her pain with alcohol...)*

## Wrongdoer #2: Impersonal Labels and Human Realities

Impersonal labels I have given this person while in a state of unforgiveness:

Today I'll start thinking of this person in terms of their *humanity, describing them as*:

## Wrongdoer #3: Impersonal Labels and Human Realities

Impersonal labels I have given this person while in a state of unforgiveness:

Today I'll start thinking of this person in terms of their *humanity, describing them as*:

**Wrongdoer #4: Impersonal Labels and Human Realities**

Impersonal labels I have given this person while in a state of unforgiveness:

Today I'll start thinking of this person in terms of their *humanity, describing them as*:

Step 2—Choose to Stop Seeking Vengeance

*Remember, the right to get even comes with a price tag: You spend a lot of sideways energy, which is your energy. Seeking revenge is like trying to run a marathon with a 100 lb. rucksack on your back. You'll finish last, crossing the finish line beat up and exhausted.*

**Things I've been doing to get revenge and seek a little vengeance:**

**Things I could be doing instead, that move me closer to doing/having the things I really want in the next 6-12 months (i.e., living an extraordinary life):**

Step 3: Choose New Feelings About the Person You're Forgiving

*Review the Humanity labels you gave your wrongdoers in Step 1 above.*

*Now is the time to choose to feel differently about your wrongdoers, guided by their humanity.*

**Wrongdoer #1:**

Before giving myself the **gift** of forgiveness, I allowed myself to feel this way towards this person: *(Examples: Rage, hate, disgust...)*

In light of this person's humanity, I choose to revise my feelings towards him/her. I will sincerely pray/hope for these positive things to happen, and I'll sincerely wish them well:

*(Example—a co-worker who is rude and hostile: "I pray that she'll get relief from the pain of her divorce, and find happiness. I sincerely wish her well.)*

**Wrongdoer #2:**

Before giving myself the **gift** of forgiveness, I allowed myself to feel this way towards this person:

In light of this person's humanity, I choose to revise my feelings towards him/her. I will sincerely pray/hope for these positive things to happen, and I'll sincerely wish them well:

**Wrongdoer #3:**

Before giving myself the *gift* of forgiveness, I allowed myself to feel this way towards this person:

In light of this person's humanity, I choose to revise my feelings towards him/her. I will sincerely pray/hope for these positive things to happen, and I'll sincerely wish them well:

**Wrongdoer #4:**

Before giving myself the *gift* of forgiveness, I allowed myself to feel this way towards this person:

In light of this person's humanity, I choose to revise my feelings towards him/her. I will sincerely pray/hope for these positive things to happen, and I'll sincerely wish them well:

Step 4: Rinse & Repeat, Remembering What Forgiveness is NOT.

## Important Reminders

☐ I'm being mindful that forgiveness is a *process,* not a one-time event.

☐ I am committed to reviewing and repeating the process above, as many times as it takes, to give myself this **gift** of forgiveness.

☐ I recognize that forgiveness is NOT: A substitute for common sense.

*I won't throw common sense out the window just because I've forgiven someone. I might forgive a drunk driver for running me over, but I wouldn't get in a car with them if they're still struggling with alcohol addiction.*

☐ I recognize that forgiveness is NOT: Re-unification with the wrongdoer.

*Reunion with a wrongdoer (if I want that) only happens when the wrongdoer is honestly sorry for what he did and can be trusted to not wrong me again. Forgiveness is something that happens in my heart. But it may not be in the best interest of anyone involved for a reunion to occur.*

☐ I recognize that forgiveness is NOT: About letting the bad conduct happen again, nor Is It about forgetting what happened.

*Back to common sense! I'll move forward cautiously in light of what I know to be true about the person. I won't open the door to bad conduct. Forgiveness doesn't require me to be a doormat.*

Who/what else would be able to aid me in this process of forgiveness and healing?

☐ A professional therapist.

☐ Regular outings with a trusted friend.

☐ A pastor, rabbi, priest, spiritual advisor.

☐ A life/business coach.

☐ Other:

Made in the USA
San Bernardino, CA
09 February 2020